Martini, Straight Up

Martini, Straight Up
The Classic American Cocktail

LOWELL EDMUNDS

THE JOHNS HOPKINS UNIVERSITY PRESS / BALTIMORE AND LONDON

© 1981, 1998 Lowell Edmunds
Printed in the United States of America on acid-free paper
First edition published 1981 by Greenwood Press as *The Silver Bullet: The Martini in American Civilization*
Revised edition 1998
9 8 7 6 5 4 3 2 1

The Johns Hopkins University Press
2715 North Charles Street
Baltimore, Maryland 21218-4363
The Johns Hopkins Press Ltd., London
www.press.jhu.edu

"The Last Martini" by Daniel Hardy is from *The Best of Bad Hemingway: Choice Entries from the Harry's Bar and American Grill Imitation Hemingway Competition,* with an introduction by George Plimpton; copyright © 1989 Harry's Bar & American Grill; reprinted by permission of Harcourt Brace & Company.

Library of Congress Cataloging-in-Publication Data will be found at the end of this book.
A catalog record for this book is available from the British Library.

ISBN 0-8018-5971-9

To Sue

CONTENTS

The Simple Messages of the Martini

The Ambiguities of the Martini

ILLUSTRATIONS

Drawings by Deborah Ellis appear on pages iii, 1, 39, and 101

PREFACE TO THE REVISED EDITION

THE MARTINI brings back memories—good ones, and, alas, as the years pass, some bad ones, too. I remember Harry's Bar in 1956—the pyramid of stemmed Martini glasses, each full of cracked ice, that Roger built in anticipation of cocktail hour. When an order for a Martini came, he would mix the drink, dump the ice out of a glass, and pour in the marvelous mixture. The sight delighted my young eyes and would delight my old eyes too if they could see it now. But in Harry's Bar they cannot. In April 1990, when I was teaching as *professore a contratto* at the University of Venice, I dropped in at Harry's for a Martini, as had been my wont whenever I was in Venice. The bartender reached down to a refrigerator below the bar, pulled out what looked like an oversized shot glass encrusted with frost, and set it down in front of me. A ready-mixed Martini in a dripping shot glass, tasting, of course, like the inside of a refrigerator, and it cost, as I remember, the equivalent of $8.

As Hugo Williams said, "What a strange coincidence it is that everything always changes for the worse during the course of a single lifetime." In my experience of the Martini outside of my own home, how often have I seen the ravages of time. My earlier playfulness as a Martini writer is no longer possible. The persona of Martini purist that I adopted in the first edition of this book—or, as Werner Dannhauser, a reviewer in the *American Spectator,* called it, "Martini elitist"—is no longer a persona. It is the real I.

It is difficult, in this state of mind, to write the engaging preface that I ought to write. So let me begin by taking back some of the unpleasant things I said in the preface to the first edition. I remove the curse that I placed on the editors of publications that refused to print my queries about the Martini. May they *not* die—may no one die, as Sherwood Anderson did—by swallowing the toothpick from a Martini. I have now read B. H. Kean's account of Anderson's autopsy: "The fatal toothpick had passed through the stomach and small bowel, gotten caught in a diverticulum, and perforated it, so that the liquid stool poured into the closed chamber of the belly, producing large pockets of pus around the bladder." In his book *M.D.: One Doctor's Adventures among the Famous and Infamous from the Jungles of Panama to a Park Avenue Practice* (1990), Dr. Kean tells the story at length, showing how he established that the fatal toothpick had come from a Martini.

The editor of the *New York Times Book Review* was one of those who lived for nearly twenty years under my curse. But, strangely, he or she or a successor came to publish that curse. Here is how it happened. On

April 15, 1990, John Maxwell Hamilton published an essay in the *Book Review* on the authorial preface. His main point was authors' insincerity. He could not find a single example of genuine frankness. Then, on May 13, the *Book Review* printed a letter from William S. Moran, who pointed out Hamilton's omission of my preface, which would have provided him with the example that he could not find, and Moran quoted my curse. I leave it to Jacques Derrida to explain how the curse, inspired by the silencing of the query, was cited because of its omission, or as an omission, and is now cited by me in its cited form in Moran, or rather re-cited, because I have already cited it in its original source, which was I, no, my persona, in the preceding paragraph. As the present, real I, I was intending to remove the curse, but I am not sure that I am succeeding.

But if I adopt a hortatory stance and give some advice, perhaps I can restore my identity and be fully present to the reader. What I said in the preface to the first edition about how to mix a Martini still stands. Now I should like to concentrate on the olive, about which I have written a lot in the introduction, apropos of the so-called return of the Martini in the 1990s. People think that the olive is the natural garnish of the Martini. As the Witch of Grafton said, I'm going to tell them something they won't like. In the first place, the toothpick on which the olive is usually impaled is dangerous. Dr. Kean cited an article in the *New England Journal of Medicine* that showed that Sherwood Anderson's fate is hardly unique. The full reference will be found in "Theory, Method, and Bibliography" at the end of this book. I know that the fear of death is not going to stop people from rash behavior, so let me give a stronger reason for not using olives: They ruin the taste of the drink. I mean the traditional straight-up Martini. Even at 3.5 ounces, it will still be warmer at the end than at the beginning, and as it becomes warmer, offensive, foreign flavors have a chance to ruin the drink. The olive or its brine and, still worse, the pimiento or other stuffing produce such flavors. Once upon a time, chic bars did not put olives in Martinis. In the introduction to this book I cite a 1934 *Esquire* article on this matter. I agree with its author, who says, "With me, the man who first placed an olive in a Martini is no more popular than the guy who introduced barbed wire to Texas." The only garnish I have encountered that makes a Martini taste better as it becomes warmer is fresh mint, which was recommended to me by Walter Kaiser. As for the twist, I can only repeat what I said in the earlier preface. The lemon peel should be twisted over the surface of the drink, for the sake of the oil in the rind, not smeared on the edge of the glass.

Now to be conciliatory, I want to add that an olive is not bad as an hors d'oeuvre, to eat while you are drinking a Martini. Three French olives that I recommend are the Niçoise, the Picholine, and the Green

Lucque. The slightly roasted Moroccan ones sprinkled with rosemary are also good. These four complement each other as well as the drink. It is pleasant to have a couple of each, and this amount of olives is almost a meal in itself for certain Martini drinkers. (See the joke about the WASP's seven-course banquet in Simple Message 3.)

And now to my thanks, which have to be really real. Because the persona of the preface to the first edition was deemed sincere—because, oddly, of the curse—it seems that the best thing to do is to revert to that persona, that earlier Martini writer whose psycho-physiological activity somehow persists in this present effort. I constantly relied on the reference librarians in Alexander Library at Rutgers: Stephanie Bartz, Ilona Caparros, Boyd Collins, Joseph P. Consoli, Emily Fabiano, Mary Fetzer, Ellen Gilbert, Ron Jantz, Linda Langschied, Kevin Mulcahy, Stanley D. Nash, Susan Peters, Myoung Wilson, and Miles Yoshimura. The director of Information Services at the Center of Alcohol Studies Library at Rutgers, Penny Page, and her assistant Sara Harrington not only kindly helped me when I was in the library but remembered me and saved things for me that they thought I could use. Carol Paszamant (Citation/Location Center, Rutgers University Libraries) made valiant efforts to find the fugitive bartender's manuals about which I have written in "Theory, Method, and Bibliography" at the end of this book.

The Martini glass was a project unto itself. Jane Shadel Spillman at the Corning Museum of Glass did a lot of research on my behalf, and the material for Figure 11 is almost entirely owing to her. Susan Frantz at the Corning Museum was also very helpful to me. I also thank William Ayres (The Museums at Stony Brook), Patricia Barroll (Carillon Importers, Ltd.), Dena Cook (Lalique), Nicholas M. Dawes, Steve Van Dyk (Cooper-Hewitt Museum), Silvie Jouen (Lalique), Leslie Piña (Ursuline College), and Martin Shapiro (Postcards International). My conversations and correspondence with Ulysses G. Dietz, curator of Decorative Arts at the Newark Museum, finally galvanized me into making the statement on the Martini glass that appears in the appendix.

Others helped on other subjects: R. W. Apple Jr. (*New York Times*), Patricia Barroll (Carillon Importers, Ltd.), William K. Beatty (Frances E. Willard Memorial Library, Evanston, Ill.), John Belton (Rutgers), Donald Byers (Hotel Employees and Restaurant Employees International Union), Paul Cartledge (Cambridge University), Irwin Chusid, John W. Crowley (Syracuse University), Susan Edmunds, Heyward Ehrlich (Rutgers), Sam Elworthy (Princeton University Press), Richard Faith (Hotel Employees and Restaurant Employees International Union), Samara Farber (Kratz and Co., Inc.), Jill Frisch (*New Yorker*), Robert Genis (National Gemstone Corporation), Lee A. Ghajar, Robert Hammond (*The Bottom Line*), Harriet Hansen, Karen Klaiber (Rutgers), James W. Leyerzapf (Eisenhower Archives), Dan and Jan Longone (Wine and Food Library, Ann Arbor), Shirley McCombe (Small Point Club), Peter Moody, Joseph and Susan Nevadunsky, David J. Nordloh (Indiana University), Josh Ober (Princeton University), William O'Neill (Rutgers), David Oshinsky (Rutgers), Stephen Parks (Beinecke Library, Yale University), Jessie Randall (Library Company of Philadelphia), Naomi Rood (Princeton University), Kenneth W. Rose (Rockefeller Archive Center), Fred Schreiber (E. K. Schreiber Books), Michael Shinagel (Harvard University Extension), Ruth Sloan (Palo Alto–Stanford Heritage), Adolph L. Soens, Eric Spilker, Hans Surber, Roger Van Eeghen (De Beers), Emily Vosburg (Bowling Green State University), Nach Waxman (Kitchen Arts and Letters, New York), Kenneth W. Wheeler (Rutgers), and Jack White. I also thank my fellow Martini-researchers, Barnaby Conrad III, William Grimes (*New York Times*), and Max Rudin (Library of America). Their writings on the Martini and their responses to my questions over the past several months have been a tremendous help. Grimes sent me extensive comments on an earlier version of the introduction.

Special thanks to Leah Edmunds and Adrienne Mayor. The former did research for me in the Library of Congress in Washington and in the Boston Public Library; contributed an illustration; and pointed me toward a rather thorough reorganization of large parts of the first edition. The latter's detailed comments have improved style and substance in dozens of places, and I have even at times borrowed her words. Some of her questions await further thought and research.

Highland Park, N.J.
October 1997

PREFACE TO THE FIRST EDITION

THIS STUDY BEGAN as a collection of Martini recipes, which itself began quite by chance when I noticed some peculiarities in the Martini recipe in the 1943 edition of *The Joy of Cooking*. In the course of time, it occurred to me that one could write a history not only of the drink itself but of its role in American social history. So I began to look for evidence in literature, advertising, and the other sources which I have discussed in the Bibliographical and Methodological Essay. After I had amassed a certain amount of evidence, it was obvious to me that a history would be impossible without several more years of work. The evidence I had, however, seemed adequate for another sort of discussion, the one here presented. This discussion is not historical in approach, nor is it literary, although I believe that one could make a study of the Martini in American fiction and poetry. Nor have I been primarily concerned with the motivations of individual Martini-drinkers or of classes of Martini-drinkers. I have approached the Martini as a symbol or, better, a sign. Insofar as possible, I have asked not what Martini-drinkers and others have said about the Martini but what the Martini has said to or about them.

It was once the fashion in writing prefaces to name the person "without whose help this book could not have been written." In the case of the present effort, there is no one such person who could be named. One does research on the Martini not only by sitting alone in a library but by questioning scores or hundreds of people in various places. My debts of gratitude are therefore unusually numerous, and many or most of them are to persons with whom I have corresponded but whom I have never met. I might add that, in the course of my research, if it deserves this name, I discovered a law of correspondence. *In both the academic and the business worlds, the more important the person, the sooner he or she answers a letter.* In the academic, assistant professors are the only ones who do not answer their mail at all; associate professors are prompter, professors still prompter, and deans are the promptest of all (I am speaking of correspondence directed outside the university).

Despite what I said about research on the Martini, I would still, if forced to rank those who helped me, assign the first place to the reference librarians in Widener Library at Harvard University. Sheila Hart, head of public services and chief reference librarian, has helped me with various projects over the years, but never more than with the Martini, her own appreciation of which is considerable. Her associates, Barry Guthary, Marion Schoon, and Andrea Schulman, not only responded to my pleas for help with their usual patience and expertise but also supplied me with material on the Martini from their own reading and observation. In this context, I must also thank my old friend Edward Doctoroff, the head of circulation in Widener, and Francis Cox, a veritable Prince of Serendip.

I cannot continue without saying that I believe that the conventions of the preface should be expanded to allow authors to cast blame on those who have hindered their research. I should like to blame the editors of *Notes and Queries* for rejecting the extremely concise and dignified query on the Martini I sent them and I should also like to blame the editor of the *New York Times Book Review* for failing to print my author's query. May these editors find that their gin has turned to gasoline or may they drink too many Martinis and then swallow a toothpick, as Sherwood Anderson is said to have done.

But now to my catalogue of thanks. Like the ancient poet, I call upon the Muses to aid my memory. Tell me how many came to the aid of the Martini! And you, Dionysus, who have often befuddled, now strengthen my power of recollection!

Richard Ingber was able to supply more references to the Martini in literature than anyone else I consulted. John Doxat, the author of the first book on the Martini, and John Stace, editor of *DCL Gazette* (the staff magazine of the Distillers Co., Ltd., Edinburgh), corresponded with me on particular problems. Since, in my experience, businessmen tend not to be much interested in the historical or other nonpractical aspects of their affairs, I am especially grateful for all the help I received from the Etablissements Noilly Prat & Cie and from Thomas G. Cockerill of Heublein. Steve L. Barsby of the Distilled Spirits Council of the U.S., Inc., gave me good advice at the beginning of my research. Professor Scott Donaldson took the trouble to provide me with information on Hemingway's Martini drinking. It was material that, as it happened, I did not use; but I am grateful all the same. I hope someday to publish a directory of illustrious Martini-drinkers, with suitable anecdotal notes. Peter Tamony, the expert on American folk speech, shared with me his voluminous collection of references to the Martini in newspapers. George Bason and Warren L. Call helped me to procure certain early bartender's manuals. In passing, I express the hope that a collector of such books— there must be one somewhere—will read these words (and the complaints I have expressed in the Bibliographical and Methodological Essay) and be moved to write to me. It was a pleasure to correspond with, and, in the case of the second named, to meet, my fellow bacchanologists, Donald J. Gonzales and Richard Barksdale Harwell. As in several other cases, I say nothing more about them here, because I have referred to them in the text or notes of my study.

Mary C. Geisler of Hammacher Schlemmer and Ann Holbrook of Gorham Textron supplied me with the photographs of the Vermouth dropper and the Martini spike that appear as illustrations in the text. Several persons answered questions on particular subjects: Mary Augusta Aiken, Robert Burchfield, Malcolm Cowley, M. F. K. Fisher, Robert Kibele, Florence Leeds, Giorgio Lolli, Marcus A. McCorison, Ruth Schorer, Howard M. Teichmann, and Jeffrey Thomas. Paul Nyeland's great generosity will be obvious from the text and one of the illustrations. My sister-in-law, Rebecca Frischkorn, sent me a never-ending stream of Martiniana from magazines that I do not usually read. Donald Carne-Ross and Richard Martin gave me useful advice on the style and organization of the first draft, the revision of which was ultimately guided by the astute comments of Robert H. Walker. I relied on the help of several librarians besides those already named: Charlotte Doudell (Santa Clara, California County Library), Michelle Leiser and Florian J. Shasky (The Stanford University Libraries), Richard Dillon (Sutro Library, San Francisco), Lois Farrell and Irene Moran (Bancroft Library, University of California, Berkeley), Karen Webster and Diana Smith (library of the Distilled Spirits Council of the U.S., Inc.), and Edel Raith (San Francisco Public Library).

I conclude my catalogue of thanks with a bare list of those who were kind enough to answer particular questions. They will forgive me, I trust, for my failure to specify their contributions: Maynard A. Amerine, Carlos Baker, George J. Becker, Michael Bell, Rex Burbank, Daniel Clift, Keith J. Fennimore, Melvin J. Friedman, Maud Gleason, Malcolm Goldstein, Richard H. Goldstone, Sheldon Grebstein, M. E. Grenander, Theodore L. Gross, Leslie Halliwell, Samuel Hazo, J. P. Hennessey, Edwin P. Hoyt, Walter Kaiser, Joseph I. Killorin, Peter Kranz, Earle Labor, Richard Layman, Richard Lehan, James F. Light, James Lundquist, Jack B. Moore, Patrick Morrow, H. P. Olmo, Walton R. Patrick, John Pilkington, William Randel, Robert Renehan, Judith Humphrey Shaw, R. W. Stallman, Wallace Stegner, and Stanley M. Ulanoff. In the final stages of the preparation of the manuscript, the help of Mrs. Lillian Reisman was of inestimable value.

It is odd and perhaps even unprecedented that a scholar should conclude a preface with a plea for his health and safety, but I know that, as a result of the publication of this monograph, I shall be offered innumerable Martinis. I also know that most of them will be downright poisonous or otherwise unacceptable. Therefore, I should like to take the unusual step of stating in advance the minimum requirements for any Martini that shall be served me.

In the first place, the Martini on the rocks is an abomination, and must be classed with fast foods, rock and roll, snowmobiles, acid rain, polyester fabrics, supermarket tomatoes, and books printed on toilet paper as a symptom of anomie. My Martini shall be served "straight up" in a thoroughly chilled, stemmed glass. The gin, but not the vermouth, which is supposed to be aromatic, shall have been chilled before mixing, and the gin and vermouth shall be stirred or shaken—I don't care which—with good ice. "Good" means made from spring water, or, failing that, Perrier or the like. There should be very slight dilution of the drink with water—it has a smoothing effect.

The first requirement, then, is that the drink be very cold. The second is that the vermouth be one of the three possible brands, none of which is domestic. The proportions can vary from 4:1 to 8:1. Here I'll make some concessions to your taste, and, anyway, it depends in part on the proof of the gin. Most American gin is now 80 proof. That came about a couple of years ago, when the cost of the grain from which gin is distilled went up. My favorite gin is made in England and is 94 proof, but there are several gins that will produce an acceptable Martini. The temperature and the vermouth are what usually go wrong. If to a tepid Martini made with vermouth that tastes like hand lotion you add a stale, briny olive, or any garnish of strange flavor, no gin in the world can succeed.

Instead of a garnish in the drink, a piece of lemon rind shall be twisted over the surface of the Martini so that the lemon oil is extruded onto its surface; and then the lemon rind shall be discarded. It is discouraging to see these young would-be bartenders wiping the rim of the Martini glass with a hunk of lemon peel, the yellow side out, so that they smear the glass with the noisome odor of the white inner rind. And then they plop this object, usually with a few vesicles of lemon flesh clinging to it, into the drink, and imagine that they have done something clever. The only thing your bartender will do right, although it's for the wrong reason, is serve you a small Martini. This drink should indeed be small—2½ ounces is a good size—since it is better to drink two cold Martinis than one Martini the second half of which is tepid.

Finally, if I seem to have asked too much, then let me offer you the Martini, and here it is.

Cambridge, Mass.
December 1979

INTRODUCTION

B ERNARD DE VOTO called it the "supreme American gift to world culture," and H. L. Mencken said that it was "the only American invention as perfect as a sonnet."[1] FDR served a Martini to Stalin at the Teheran Conference in 1943 and asked him how he liked it. "Well, all right," the Russian said, "but it is cold on the stomach."[2] Stalin's successor was served a stronger Martini than the rather bland sort that FDR mixed. Khrushchev called it "the U.S.A.'s most lethal weapon."[3]

The Martini is the premier American cocktail. It is a permanent fixture of American life, of the American imagination, of America's image in the rest of the world. But its consumption, like that of other commodities, is cyclical. At the time of the first edition of this book (1981), the Martini was in eclipse. As I did the research for this revised edition, I saw the Martini everywhere—in movie advertisements, on the jewel boxes of CDs, in magazines. Strolling around SoHo on a summer evening, I saw Martinis on every bar. How did I know it was the Martini? The glass told me.

This already much-noticed "return of the Martini" prompts three questions. Where did it return from? In what form has it returned? Where did the Martini come from in the first place?

The last question first: It was invented in the United States of the 1870s and came into its own in the Gilded Age. Let's imagine a drink consisting of two main ingredients, gin and vermouth, served chilled and with a garnish—say, an olive—in a stemmed glass. Until the middle of the twentieth century or beyond, this was the Martini. For some, it still is. Well on in life, probably in the 1920s, this drink came to be served more or less exclusively in a particular glass, the bowl of which had straight edges. The glass with the triangular profile became part of the drink's identity. This glass and the name "Martini" have never parted company.

Like many American institutions, the Martini did not easily survive the 1960s. The following decade brought concerns of health into the sphere of drinking. Light beer, mineral water, and white wine replaced cocktails. The Martini, such as it was, was served on the rocks, and vodka was more likely than gin to be its backbone. The change to vodka had started in the early 1950s.[4] The glass was no longer the stemmed one but an Old Fashioned glass. This change of vessel left a trace in the American language. To order the earlier cocktail—that is, chilled, in a stemmed glass, whether with gin or with vodka—one used a retronym: "straight-up Martini" or Martini "straight up." The expression was also shortened to "Martini up."

So the drink itself changed, and it was drunk in a different glass. But the Martini's image remained intact. It was still, in the world's eyes, the premier American cocktail, and it still meant everything it had meant earlier in the United States. Much of this book is devoted to an analysis and description of what it meant and means. But the slippage between the drink itself and its image is what made possible the return of the Martini.

Its return in the 1990s is the return of the image. Only a few diehards still drink the old straight-up gin Martini, which Robert Donohoe of Athens, Ohio, calls the American Standard Dry Martini, after the one prescribed in a brochure of the American Standards Association in 1966 (see "Historical Background of the Ambiguities"). Donohoe organized the American Standard Dry Martini Club in the winter of 1990–91 and issued a newsletter, "The Martini Hotline," for seven years. The very first number struck an elegiac note: "Right now it's tough to find a stout-hearted drinker of the ASDM cocktail. I mean, it's getting lonesome out there. I hope those of us who are left can continue to enjoy the ASDM, at least in a home setting, but, as we fade out of the picture, who will take our place?"

But some as yet unformulated law seems to say that as the power of the thing diminishes, the power of its image increases. The return of the Martini has seen its image unfold energetically in several dimensions. Most obviously, the Martini becomes a subject of reflection and discourse, as in this book, and in other writings—William Grimes's chapter on the Martini in his cultural history of the cocktail (1993); Barnaby Conrad's *The Martini* (1995); Max Rudin's essay, "'There Is Something about a Martini,'" in *American Heritage* (1997).[5] The Martini is for all of us not just a drink, perhaps not even a drink at all, but an intriguing aspect of American history and culture.

As for the return of the Martini in the social life of the 1990s, the glass has done the work. The traditional glass with v-shaped profile is everywhere. A plastic version is available. It is depicted in garish colors on cocktail napkins sold by Pier 1 Imports, with the word "Martini" printed on two of the margins. One can purchase the familiar profile in the form of a refrigerator magnet, or a neon sign for the home bar.[6] One can even select a typeface based on the Martini glass.[7] In response to the new popularity of the form, Lalique introduced a Martini glass in the fall of 1997 (Plate 1).[8] Its traditionality extends even to its packaging in sets of two, which implies what I discuss, in Ambiguity 2, as the Martini-of-the-relationship and the conjugal Martini.

But what will be served in this handsome glass? Not the straight-up gin or vodka Martini. Bars all across the land have Martini menus offering concoctions that bear no resemblance to the traditional drink. The

Dragon Lounge in Corpus Christi, Texas, offers a dozen "specialty Martinis." These include April's Martini (Godiva chocolate liqueur, Frangelico, and an orange twist), the Cosmopolitan (Absolut Vodka, Cointreau, orange juice, and a splash of cranberry juice), and the Blue Skyy (Skyy Vodka, blue curaçao, and an orange twist). But why limit the contents to drink? The traditional glass is now also used to serve food. Writing in the *New York Times*, Florence Fabricant offers her readers recipes for "Salmon Tartar 'Martini'" and "Ecuadorean Ceviche 'Martini.'" She observes, "In restaurants, the martini glass has become an all-purpose item, like the soup plate."[9]

The Martini—again, the glass and the name—has become an icon in the social rituals of young single persons. In a movement sometimes called Cocktail Nation (in mockery of Woodstock Nation), they don tuxedos and sheath dresses, go to bars decorated in the style of 1950s lounges and ballrooms, dance to swing music, and, when they are not dancing, listen to old recordings of Dean Martin and Tony Bennett. The music of the bands performing for this taste is called "space age bachelor pad music,"[10] or simply "lounge." The spokesman of the movement is Michael "the Millionaire" Cudahy, guitarist of the band Combustible Edison. He has issued two manifestos of Cocktail Nation. The first began, "Calling all swingers," and ended with the injunction, "BE FABULOUS." And the Martini? In an article on the lounge scene in *Allure* magazine, Judy Bachrach told young women, "MARTINIS ARE A MUST."[11]

The drink appears in abundance in a central document of the movement, the film *Swingers* (1996), directed by Doug Liman. It is about aspiring actors and actresses in Los Angeles and was in fact written by one of them, Jon Favreau. He also plays the role of Mike, who is trying to recover from the breakup of a long relationship. His friends, principally Trent (Vince Vaughn), take him to trendy nightspots where they hope that he'll score. In one of his failed attempts, Mike introduces himself to a girl at a bar, Nikki (Brooke Langton), who has a Martini glass in front of her and is holding a toothpick on which six or more olives are impaled. She is fast gobbling them up, and Mike instructs the bartender to bring her more. The Martini and the olives are just props; the point of the scene is that Mike will fail again. But one still notices the use of the Martini as a source of food. The American Standard Dry Martini must contain a single olive, and a traditionalist like Donohoe does not eat it.[12] It is there for looks. For the young Martini-drinker in the film, however, it is there to be eaten and the drink is there for looks, as a purely visual icon of style.

Nikki and the others in *Swingers* are the potential readers of Anistatia R. Miller and Jared M. Brown's *Shaken Not Stirred: A Celebration of the Martini* (1997)[13] or of the same authors' website, http://www.martinis

.com/key/. They might also be the students of Samara Farber (Kratz and Co., Inc.) and Tricia Barroll (Carillon Importers, Ltd.) who conduct Martini seminars in various cities in the United States. Miller and Brown's book is a didactic work that tells young people not only how to mix Martinis but what (beyond olives) to eat with them, what clothes to wear, and what music to listen to. It even provides instructions on how to do the tango. Robert Donohoe, who told the *New York Times* in 1996 that a vodka Martini is not a Martini, would be alarmed to learn of the categories of Martini for which Miller and Brown offer recipes: Fruit Martinis, Dessert Martinis, Spice and Cajun Martinis, Flavored-Vodka Martinis, and Martinis Built for Two (Passionate Elixirs).[14] These would appear to be the kinds of Martini drunk by the characters in the 1997–98 season of the television series *Melrose Place*. An entertainment guide promised, "For the *Swingers* taste, the cast will swill martinis instead of sipping beer."[15]

The Martini glass is not just an icon in the hands of the young. It has also returned in another way in the 1990s. Its functionality becomes un-important, and it becomes an artifact that can be redesigned on purely aesthetic principles. This visual rethinking of the glass has taken place across a broad range of styles, from craft to deconstructive. As an exam-ple of the former, I have included the Martini glasses of Michael Jaross, a Seattle glassblower (Plate 2). In response to my question about the for-mal origin of these glasses, he replied, "Yes, I did have the classic mar-tini 'cone' in mind." But, he continued,

> I'm more interested in pure form and color. Since I prefer to stick with functional designs, the "Martini" gave me a point of departure to play with, but one which has a certain cachet for the buyer. Factory Martini glasses tend to be austere and thin, while I added body to mine to sup-port more visual elements and more color, separating the piece from fac-tory work, giving it more character, thus identifying it as "artist-made." Of course, I left the bowl transparent as most drinkers prefer to see what they are imbibing.[16]

Jaross gives a nod to functionality, but at the other end of the stylistic spectrum from him one finds "Martini" art objects from which it would be impossible to drink a Martini.

Several of the nine glasses that have appeared since 1990 in the ad-vertising campaign for Bombay Sapphire Gin come under this descrip-tion. Hilton McConnico's is a deconstructive reading of the traditional form (Plate 3), not a new design for a Martini glass. It is a postmodern gesture that retains a certain ironic affection for its historical source. McConnico starts, I think, from the impression of perfect balance, bowl on stem, that the traditional glass gives. He creates a new kind of balance by elongating the stem and bending it into an asymmetrical curve that reaches high above the bowl. The stem now makes contact with the base at the apex of the curve. At one end of the curve is the bowl, at the other a glass olive. The two masses, bowl and olive, balance the curved stem on the base, but in such a way that the base is no longer directly under the bowl. The olive is no longer a dead weight in the drink but has, in its new, inedible, purely formal treatment, a dynamic role. It is no longer elevated by the glass but keeps the glass elevated. McConnico's glass seems to say, "The olive was only there for looks; let's have it do something to earn its keep."

The base and the bowl are clear; the stem is blue. The color links McConnico's glass with the postmodern Martini of the 1990s. The blue Martini, achieved by the use of blue curaçao, is available not only at the Dragon Lounge in Corpus Christi but all across the United States. "I love blue Martinis. It's like the fifties and the nineties all mixed up together," says a woman in a *New Yorker* cartoon, articulating the new Martini's postmodern eclecticism.[17] But Robert Donohoe's name for his beloved American Standard Dry Martini is "hard white." The drink has had other similar names: "see through" and "silver bullet." "We called them silver bullets," Jerry Della Femina, the CEO of a New York advertising agency, recalled wistfully in 1989.[18] The traditional look of the drink was white or clear or silver, but not blue. The new addition of color is an ironic gesture that conforms exactly with Linda Hutcheon's definition of postmodern parody as "repetition with critical distance that allows ironic signaling of difference at the very heart of similarity." "To parody," she says, "is not to destroy the past; in fact to parody is both to enshrine the past and to question it."[19]

The prominence of the olive in McConnico's glass is another kind of postmodern gesture. In the traditional drink, the olive was a garnish that marked the drink as special, perhaps elevating the status of the gin, once a working-class drink, and complementing the glassware and all the rest of the ritual. The olive was there not to be eaten but to make a visual effect that would contribute to the larger picture, in which all the elements were saying the same thing. This redundancy of the message comes to a stop when McConnico takes the olive out of the glass and assigns it a radically new role. By intervening in this way, he calls attention to the very process of communication. He is putting on display not only a new, deconstructive Martini glass but also, and perhaps even more emphatically, the very process by which the Martini has been able to maintain its power as an image. At a practical level, Nikki was doing the same thing in the film *Swingers* when she replaced the drink with the olives. The Martini sitting in front of her is retro, yes, but her olive-munching can be seen as typical postmodern self-consciousness about symbolic communication.

Much of the history of the Martini in the 1990s, including many real persons named in this introduction and later in this book, appears in *Cold and Stiff*, a 16 mm film directed by Peter Moody of San Francisco. He calls it a "docudramedy." It is about Nick Martini, played by Paul Arensburg, who is also the co-writer. Nick is a bicycle messenger who falls in love with a retro-dressing femme fatale. To pursue her, he becomes a 1940s detective. The conceit of the film is that his transformation will succeed if he learns everything there is to know about the Martini. His education brings him into contact with every source of expertise, even a skilled maker of neon Martini signs, Bill Concannon (Plate 4). Nick thus experiences more completely than anyone else the return of the Martini.

But his real quest is for a lifestyle and thus for the *image* of the Martini, which is, as I have argued, the mode in which the Martini has returned in the 1990s. The question now arises: What is the image? This question can be translated into another one: What does the Martini communicate? The initial answer to this question, which occupies the first part of this book, is this: The Martini sends seven Simple Messages. I call these messages simple because they are binary in form (the Martini is x, it is not y, the opposite of x). They are:

MESSAGE ONE: The Martini is American—it is not European, Asian, or African
MESSAGE TWO: The Martini is urban and urbane—it is not rural or rustic
MESSAGE THREE: The Martini is a high-status, not a low-status, drink
MESSAGE FOUR: The Martini is a man's, not a woman's, drink
MESSAGE FIVE: The Martini is optimistic, not pessimistic
MESSAGE SIX: The Martini is the drink of adults, not of children
MESSAGE SEVEN: The Martini belongs to the past, not to the present

Nick's Martini, the Martini of the swingers in the film of that name, or the Martini of Anistatia R. Miller and Jared M. Brown, as a deliberately retro drink, is communicating Simple Message 7. Other accouterments of swinger style help to specify the decades, the 1940s and the 1950s. This swinger's Martini is also picking out some of the other Simple Messages, as well as yet another message, which I discuss in Part Two, namely, that the Martini is civilized. The suave retro Martini of the 1990s is part of a reaction against the punk and grunge styles, now perceived as churlish.

As deployed by the swingers, the Martini expresses the lifestyle of a particular period in the past. In the longer view that I try to take, the Martini does not belong to any decade in particular; rather, it has *always,* almost from its origin, been a drink of the past. Different persons will attach it to different decades. Writing in 1985 as a spokesman of the older generation, Donald G. Smith thought of the Martini as the drink of his father's generation.[20] Jerry Della Femina remembered the Martini as a drink of the 1960s. The Martini does not belong to any real historical period; it is simply of the past, timelessly of the past.

Further, all the Simple Messages of the Martini and also the Ambiguities discussed in Part Two belong to a synchronous system. All the messages coexist. They are always all there and have always, so to speak, constituted the Martini's image. As for Simple Message 7, the Martini would not, of course, have been a drink of the past in, say, the first decade of its existence, but at some point it acquired this connotation, and this message has since remained unchanged, like all the others.

Not all of the messages will come into play for the same person at the same time. Everyone will activate his or her own subset. For the swingers, the Martini expresses a lifestyle that belongs to an earlier time and is also "fabulous." For Della Femina too it expresses a lifestyle, but the temporal setting is different and so is the social one: it is the corporate culture of the three-Martini lunch, hardly a message that the swingers want to convey.

For the most part, use of the Martini's image is not explicitly ideological but seems innocent. The fact remains that the binary oppositions on which the Simple Messages are based include a potentially disturbing hierarchical ranking. The first term is good or superior, the second bad or inferior:

American	European, Asian, African
urban, urbane	rural, rustic
upper-class	lower-class
male	female
optimistic	pessimistic
adult	immature
past	present

The net result for the Martini is politically incorrect, to say the least. Power and the self-interest of particular persons and groups would seem to be written into the image of the Martini as a whole. I myself do not "have a problem with that," for reasons to be explained later, but I do not want to seem to dismiss the problem if someone else finds it. And someone will. Indeed, an enormous amount of work, in the humanities and social sciences, is preoccupied precisely with power and the ways in which one group exerts authority over another. My approach will be to focus on the Martini as an image—or, in semiotic terms, a sign or sign-vehicle—without going any more deeply into social contexts than a sketch of the sign requires. "Sketch" is not *sprezzatura*. This book might seem long in relation to its subject—I have been asked again and again, "How could you write a *book* on the Martini?"—but it could be much longer.

As for binary oppositions as such, no one has to believe in them any longer. The inferior terms can be shown to have left traces in the superior ones. The oppositions can be broken down. I have not chosen to perform this operation on the Simple Messages. Rather, in Part Two I take some larger messages, some larger claims of the drink, and show that they are fundamentally ambiguous. The Martini is civilized, yes, as the swingers and many before them have intended, but it is also uncivilized, the drink of loners, misfits, and alcoholics. It can be an individual, tough drink as well as a classic, sensitive one. The Ambiguities of the Martini have, by the way, persisted into the 1990s. Besides the fabulous Martini of the swingers there is also the sinister Martini of noir style, which I discuss in Ambiguity 1. From the Ambiguities it will be even clearer that I do not subscribe to the obnoxious tendencies of the Simple Messages. The Martini provides 360 degrees of opportunity for anyone who wishes to look into or through this drink. My point or points of observation will not, I hope, be confused with my opinions about what I see.

TIME LINE
THE MARTINI DECADE BY DECADE

PRESIDENTS	EVENTS, MOVEMENTS, SPIRIT OF THE TIMES	THE MARTINI
1870–1879		
U. S. Grant '69–'77	Pop. surges to 39.8 mil.	Probable decade of origin.
R. B. Hayes '77–'81	Tennis introduced into U.S. Centennial Exhibition ('76). Light bulb. Telephone.	
1880–1889		
J. A. Garfield '81	Gilded Age. Populism.	First recipes for Martini
C. A. Arthur '81–'85	Brooklyn Bridge ('83).	appear in bartender's manu-
G. Cleveland '85–'89	Coca-Cola ('86).	als ('84; '88). First recipe calling for an olive ('88).
1890–1899		
B. Harrison '89–'93	The Gay Nineties. Gibson	First reference to the Martini
G. Cleveland '93–'97	Girls. Breakfast cereals. Gold	(dry) in literature: Hidley
W. McKinley '97–'01	Rush ('97). Spanish-American War ('98).	Dhee ('96).
1900–1909		
T. Roosevelt '01–'09	Age of Reform. Wright brothers ('03). Model T ('08). Panama Canal.	Reference to the Martini becomes common. First illustration of a glass designated "Martini."
1910–1919		
W. H. Taft '09–'13	World War I ('14–'18). Women's	The Martini becomes one of
W. Wilson '13–'21	Suffrage. Prohibition begins ('19).	the standard cocktails.
1920–1929		
W. G. Harding '21–'23	Roaring Twenties. Jazz Age.	Bathtub gin fuels the Martini.
C. Coolidge '23–'29	Lindbergh's flight ('27). Crash ('29).	Women drink with men in the speakeasy.

PRESIDENTS	EVENTS, MOVEMENTS, SPIRIT OF THE TIMES	THE MARTINI
1930–1939		
H. Hoover[M] '29–'33 F. D. Roosevelt[M] '33–'45	Depression. Repeal ('33). New Deal. Rise of Fascism in Europe.	FDR as chief priest of the Martini-ritual. The glass with the v-shaped cone. Nick and Nora Charles in *The Thin Man* ('34).
1940–1949		
H. S. Truman '45–'53	World War II. Atomic bomb ('45). Cold War begins.	The Martini as the drink of statesman and executive. DeVoto's essays on the Martini.
1950–1959		
D. D. Eisenhower '53–'61	Ike Age. Korean War ('50–'53). TV. Rock and roll. Silent Generation. Beat Generation.	Beginnings of the dryness fetish. Vodka begins to replace gin. The macho Martini (Ernest Hemingway; James Bond).
1960–1969		
J. F. Kennedy '61–'63 L. B. Johnson '63–'69	Camelot. Vietnam. The youth rebellion. Beatles' U.S. tour ('64). Woodstock Nation.	The decline of the traditional Martini.
1970–1979		
R. M. Nixon[M] '69–'74 G. R. Ford[M] '74–'77 J. E. Carter '77–'81	Watergate ('72–'74). Fall of Saigon ('75). ERA. Elvis dies ('77). Hostage crisis ('79).	The "three-Martini lunch" denounced by Carter. White wine and Perrier replace cocktails. The surviving Martini: vodka on the rocks.
1980–1989		
R. Reagan '81–'89	Me Decade. Reagan Revolution. Personal computer. Gorbachev; glasnost; perestroika.	Sales of carbonated mineral water rise to 700 mil. gallons by '84. First edition of *The Silver Bullet* ('81).
1990–1999		
G. Bush[M] '89–'93 W. J. Clinton '93–	Persian Gulf War ('90). Generation X. Internet.	Return of the Martini in retro culture. Bizarre flavored Martinis. Books and serious articles on the Martini appear.

[M] = Martini drinker:

HOOVER: David Burner, *Herbert Hoover: A Public Life* (New York: Knopf, 1979), 218–19: "From the 1930's onward, he drank martinis ritualistically ('stirring them to the right'), insisting on a larger glass late in life when his doctor limited him to one. The cocktail hour was his favorite time; 'the pause,' he called it, 'between the errors and trials of the day and the hopes of the night.'"

FDR: See "Historical Background of the Ambiguities."

NIXON: David Butwin, "Nixon in Rebozoland," *Saturday Review*, 8 Mar. 1969, 109: "'If he is a connoisseur of anything,' a Nixon observer told me, 'it is martinis. He is very particular about the brand of gin—he prefers Beefeater—and the way it's mixed.'"

FORD: Hugh Sidey, "Gerald Ford's Old Clothes," *Time*, 28 Oct. 1974, 17; Marjorie Hunter, in an article on Air Force One, "Top of the Line in Magic Carpets," *New York Times*, sec. 10 (Travel), 25 Dec. 1977, 1: "President Gerald Ford always had two large martinis before meals and two scoops of butter pecan ice cream for dessert."

BUSH: Letter from George Bush to Barnaby Conrad III, 14 Feb. 1994: "It is well known that I like a dry vodka martini, shaken, with a twist of lemon."

The Simple Messages
of the Martini

The Martini is American—
it is not European, Asian, or African

America, when he first visited it in 1958, impressed him . . . as a land of milk and martinis. — GEORGE WATSON, 1997

A MERICAN PRESIDENTS wielded the Martini in meetings with their Soviet counterparts in the 1940s and 1950s. The cocktail also played a role in less serious diplomatic games. In May 1950 Secretary of State Dean Acheson went by way of Paris to a meeting of NATO's Council of Ministers in London. He intended, as a courtesy, to hold informal talks with the French foreign minister, Robert Shuman, in advance of the meeting in London. Shuman surprised him by outlining a plan to place the entire French-German production of coal and steel under a joint authority, and he swore Acheson to secrecy. It therefore happened that when Ernest Bevin, the English secretary of state for foreign affairs, learned of the plan, he believed that Acheson had deliberately concealed it from him. Bevin flew into a rage, and only with great difficulty were the former good relations between him and Acheson restored. But, says Acheson, "Bevin had his revenge." Shortly before Acheson's return to the United States, Bevin invited him to drop by at the end of the day:

> "I know you like a Martini," said Ernie, "and it's hard to get a good one in London." Something was definitely afoot. I expressed guarded anticipation. At Bevin's signal, an ancient butler began operations at a sideboard. With growing disbelief I watched him pour into a tumbler one-third gin, one-third Italian vermouth, and one-third water without ice, then bring the tumbler to me on a tray.

Ernie was observing all this with what he thought was a Mona Lisa smile—but was more like the grin of a schoolboy up to deviltry.

It was clear that I could never drink this horror if I tasted it. The only course was to take it in one gulp, or call "uncle." I chose the former, and down it went.

"Have another," Ernie almost commanded.

"No, thank you," I said. "No one could make another just like that one."[1]

In the 1990s, it was still difficult to get a good Martini in London. Christopher Fildes wrote in the *Spectator*, "The two dollar martini has brushed against my lips like an angel's kiss. At teatime on Monday the magic figure flashed up on the screen: £1 = $2. It was my signal to fly the Atlantic and lap up martinis while such a mad exchange rate lasted."[2] The Queen Mother was more efficient. Instead of going to the United States, she went to an American in England. R. W. Apple Jr., now Washington bureau chief of the *New York Times*, attended a dinner at Fleur Cowles's in London in the early 1980s when he was on assignment there. Another of the guests was the Queen Mother. During cocktails a butler approached Apple and said that the Queen Mother would like to see him:

> "God, I thought", recalls Apple, "I have committed some giant gaff". She said, "Young man, I take it from your accent that you are an American", and I said, "Guilty". "I presume, then, that you know how to make a dry Martini". I said, "Yes, ma'am", and she said, "Go with this man to the kitchen and show him how. Eleven to one, please".[3]

Any American, or at least any American important enough to be at the same dinner party with the Queen Mother, will know how to make a dry Martini.

The American Martini-drinker, going to Europe, is in trouble. The impossibility of getting a dry Martini in any but the best hotels in the largest European capitals is an oft-repeated traveler's tale. You asked for gin and vermouth and got them mixed half and half, without ice, and the vermouth was red. You asked for gin and vermouth with ice, and you got one small lump of ice floating on the surface of an obscure cocktail occupying the lower regions of a tall glass.

The essayist M. F. K. Fisher devoted a whole article to the problem of ordering a dry Martini in France. She held that the Martini begins to deteriorate even while the traveler is still in transit: "The same rule applies by air and by sea: subtly and irrevocably the cocktail becomes more wine and less liquor the nearer one gets to Europe."[4] She explains that in France you must ask for "Martini-gin," pronounced "martini-zheen," and then explain the proportions of gin and vermouth and the extreme importance of ice.

European ignorance of the Martini, this time the Germans', is the basis of a joke set in the time of World War II:

> At a certain point in the War, the Germans established a top-secret school in which they trained spies for work in England. In this school, the future spies received not only the usual technical training but also a thorough education in all aspects of English culture and, at the same time, had their English accents honed to perfection. Two of the finest products of this school were chosen for a special mission and were set ashore from a U Boat on a sparsely populated coast of England. They found a road and walked into a country town. Since it was now evening, they went into a pub for dinner, and at the bar they ordered two Martinis. The bartender asked them, "Dry?" "Nein, nein," shouted one of the Germans, *"Zwei!"*

If the Martini is not European, still less is it Asian, even in the hands of Asians within the United States. Peter Anderson, a columnist for the *Boston Globe,* said, "I do not order Martinis in Chinese restaurants."[5] Writers can make dramatic capital out of the unexpectedness of the Martini in an Asian setting. A Martini-drinking scene is laid in the out-of-the-way Indian town of Amarpur in Pearl S. Buck's *Mandala* (1970). Jagat, an ex-rajah, is entertaining the American Miss Brooke Westley, who has gone to Amarpur after meeting Jagat in New Delhi. The worldly and imperious Jagat handles the cocktail hour as follows:

> "Well, what shall we have?" Jagat inquired.
>
> "Nothing for me, thank you, Jagat," the Maharani said.
>
> "Oh, come now," he exclaimed. "A martini? Ranjit has learned to make them very well."
>
> His voice was edged with impatience and she bowed her head and was silent.
>
> "A martini for the Rani," Jagat ordered, "and—why not the same for all of us? Come, come—"

Ranjit's Martini has an exotic touch, in keeping with the locale:

> [Brooke] took her glass . . . and sipped the martini. It was excellent, very dry, and with a flavor she did not know. Suddenly she decided to cast aside her shyness and be herself.
>
> "What is this flavor?" she inquired to Jagat. "It is like flowers, but not any that I know."
>
> "It is a citrus that long ago was brought here from Greece by my grandfather," Jagat replied. "It bears a small bitter fruit, but when pressed this

fruit has an extraordinary essence, a flavor that is more like flowers than fruit. We make the essence every year and bottle it—at least I suppose we do—it's more in Moti's [his wife's, the Maharani's] realm than mine, eh, my dear?"[6]

Jagat's, or Ranjit's, Martini is thus suitably Oriental, and the Martini, unexpected in India ("Ranjit has learned to make them very well"), turns out to be as exotic as the setting.

In W. S. Maugham's "The Fall of Edward Barnard" (1921), Bateman Hunter goes out to bring back his friend, Edward Barnard, who has strangely overstayed his two-year job in Tahiti. It emerges that Edward has gone native and has adopted an amoralist philosophy under the influence of an older American, Arnold Jackson, an ex-convict who has settled in Tahiti, married a native, and had a daughter by her. To Bateman's horror, he finds that Edward's only ambition is to marry this mulatto, raise coconuts, and contemplate the beauty of the islands. The truth begins to dawn on Bateman at dinner at Jackson's, where he meets the beautiful mulatto, and gets a dose of Jackson's philosophy. Dinner is preceded by cocktails, which are mixed, to Bateman's consternation, by the girl:

> It did not put him at his ease to see this sylph-like thing take a shaker and with a practiced hand mix three cocktails.
>
> "Let us have a kick in them, child," said Jackson.
>
> She poured them out and smiling delightfully handed one to each of the men. Bateman flattered himself on his skill in the subtle art of shaking cocktails and he was not a little astonished, on tasting this one, to find that it was excellent. Jackson laughed proudly when he saw his guest's involuntary look of appreciation.
>
> "Not bad, is it? I taught the child myself, and in the old days in Chicago I considered that there wasn't a bar-tender in the city that could hold a candle to me. When I had nothing better to do in the penitentiary I used to amuse myself by thinking out new cocktails, but when you come down to brass-tacks there's nothing to beat a dry Martini."
>
> Bateman felt as though someone had given him a violent blow on the funny-bone and he was conscious that he turned red and then white.[7]

One could call this the Heart of Darkness Martini. Bateman's reaction is intense because of his extreme conventionality. He does not expect a child, much less a female child, still less a female mulatto child, to be able to mix a Martini. But he is reacting more immediately to Arnold Jackson's vaunt. The ex-convict, a Martini-man—the Martini is uncivilized and tough (Ambiguities 1 and 4)—has turned the world upside down by appropriating the American cocktail for his exotic Tahitian existence.

Bateman, a young businessman, the representative of every middle-class virtue, and also a connoisseur of the Martini—the Martini is civilized and sensitive—has come to bring a fellow American home from Tahiti. He is staggered by Jackson's words because he realizes that Jackson has been able, in a stroke of miniature imperialism, to bring America to Tahiti. This realization comes to him in the form of the Martini.

A half-century later the device—child mixes Martini for Americans in the Far East—is still effective. This time we are in Korea. In the film $M*A*S*H$ (1970), which sired a television series of great longevity, the first Martini scene occurs approximately sixteen minutes into the film.[8] The army surgeons Hawkeye Pierce (Donald Sutherland) and Duke Forrest (Tom Skerritt), clad in fatigues, sitting in their scruffy tent, are drinking Martinis in stemmed glasses. The Martinis have been made by their servant, John-Ho (sometimes called Ho-John), a Korean teenager. One of their comrades (Robert Duvall), a fervent Christian who is improbably praying while they drink, disapproves of their teaching the boy to mix Martinis. The boy nervously departs saying, "I go wash clothes." Duke compliments him as he leaves: "You mix a mean Martini." (Later Hawkeye says to him, of another Martini, "Fine of kind, Ho-John.")

The Martini is urban and urbane—
it is not rural or rustic

ed encapsulates
ndidate Carter throu
. He sits down and
it?" "With or wit'
."

> The martini is a city dweller, a metropolitan. It is not to be drunk beside a mountain stream or anywhere else in the wilds, not in the open there or even indoors.—BERNARD DEVOTO, 1951

THE NINETEENTH-CENTURY COCKTAIL was unceremonious. Patsy McDonough wrote in his *Bar-keeper's Guide* of 1883, "It is a welcome companion on fishing excursions, and travelers often go provided with it on railroad journeys."[1] In an advertisement in *Puck* in the 1890s, Heublein listed the places where its "Club Cocktails," which included Martinis, might be drunk:

> For the Yacht,
> For the Sea Shore,
> For the Mountains,
> For the Fishing Party,
> For the Camping Party,
> For the Summer Hotel.

But the Martini Cocktail did not take these directions, except, perhaps, for the last. It became, instead, a city dweller. Just as the Martini, originally sweet, became dry, so it exchanged a rural for an urban identity very early on.

The most famous expression of the urbanism of the Martini is the saying once attributed to Alexander Woollcott, "Let's get out of these wet clothes and into a dry Martini." The voice is that of a city dweller. Barnaby Conrad's recent research showed that in *Every Day's a Holiday* (1937) the actor Charles Butterworth said to another character in the film, "You ought to get out of those wet clothes and into a dry martini." The screenplay was written by Mae West, who now gets the credit for this most famous Martini saying. But Billy Wilder told a columnist for the *Los Angeles Times* that Butterworth had first spoken the line of himself when he fell into a pool at the Garden of Allah, a resort in Hollywood. Mae West would have known the line, which became an instant proverb, and appropriated it for her film.[2] This attribution replaces an earlier one: Robert Benchley, or rather his press agent siring it on Benchley.[3]

A joke, perhaps the most prevalent of all Martini jokes, is built on the antithesis of city and wilderness. A sailor cast up on a desert island, a fighter pilot do▮▮▮ a hunter lost in the woods—it can be anyone isolate▮ emergency kit. The contents of the kit are, of course,▮ ▮ of olives, and perhaps even some means of producing▮ does the sailor, or whoever it may be, begin to m▮▮ several natives, or other hunters, or whoever, emerg▮ and tell him that that's no way to make a Martini. The joke depends not only upon the notorious principle of Martini-mixing, *quot homines tot sententiae,* but upon the idea that the Martini is inseparable from communal life—in effect, inseparable from the city. If Wolcott Gibbs took a silver shaker of Martinis onto the beach at Fire Island, was it not a sort of umbilical connecting him with Manhattan?[5]

The urbanism of the Martini was expressed as aptly as possible by Cole Porter in "Two Little Babes in the Wood," which was first performed in the *Greenwich Village Follies* of 1924.[6] The lyrics tell how two orphans are left to the care of a wicked uncle who abandons them in the wood in order to get their inheritance for himself. The birds build the girls a nest, and the wind sings a lullaby. A rich man in a sedan drives by and finds them. "Then he drove them down to New York town." He gives them clothes and jewelry. In a trice the girls have too many cars and too many beaux and are going to too many parties:

> They have found that the fountain of youth
> Is a mixture of gin and vermouth
> And the whole town's agreed
> That the last thing in speed
> Is the two little babes in the wood.[7]

So ends the song. The Martini is the climax of the urban transformation of the babes in the wood.

In 1976 a little-known politician from Plains, Georgia, running for the Democratic nomination for the presidency of the United States, was drawing attention to himself with a populist attack on tax loopholes.

One of his targets was badly chosen. He denounced the tax-deductible, expense-account lunch as the "$50 Martini lunch."[8] This expression somehow became "the three-Martini lunch," and the candidate's position became the butt of jokes, cartoons, editorials, and general derision. On Friday, February 17, 1978, in his press conference in Cranston, Rhode Island, President Jimmy Carter recanted, at least with regard to the Martinis: "As for the famous three-Martini lunch, I don't care how many Martinis anyone has with lunch, but I am concerned about who picks up the check."[9] He had learned that the Martini has such an established character for urbanity and refinement that anyone who attacks it identifies himself as a bumpkin.

One of the jokes that Carter inspir   this message of the Martini. A reporter following c   gh the South goes into a bar in a small rural tow   orders a Martini. The bartender asks, "With or withou   hout what?" asks the reporter. The bartender replies, "Grit

The Martini is a high-status,
not a low-status, drink

He grew up in a prominent Protestant family in upstate New York, the son of wealth on his mother's side, and although he never talked about it this way, drinking was a natural and significant part of his milieu, as much a part of the landscape he grew up in as old money and Ivy League educations. Rarefied living: there are great photographs of my father and his brother Bob during their early twenties, sitting on the patio outside their family's grand estate in upstate New York, dressed in tennis whites and sipping martinis. *Marts,* they called them. *Let's have a Mart.* — CAROLINE KNAPP, 1996

THE FAMILY ESTATE, inherited money, the Ivy League, tennis whites, Protestant religion, and one more thing to complete the picture—the Martini. Caroline Knapp's recollection of her father, Dr. Peter Knapp, is a mental picture, a composite photograph, as the juxtaposition of tennis and Martinis shows. You would not drink a Martini before tennis; afterward, you would choose something like a gin and tonic. But the Martini and tennis go together in this mental picture because these are people for whom drinking is "natural." It occupies a different place not only in their social life but also in their metabolism. Unlike us, they can drink Martinis whenever they wish. They are like the powerful criminals in movies who are always pouring themselves glassfuls of dark liquor, whiskey or brandy, from cut-glass decanters and drinking them without any visible effect. So the Knapps drank Martinis.[1] The drink was a member of the family, referred to by an affectionate nickname.[2]

Knapp's sense of the social rank of the Martini can be stated in another way. It is a white Anglo-Saxon Protestant drink, and, as such, it is a drink of the highest status. In any social ranking of ethnicity in the United States, WASPs come first and all the rest come second. I do not have to cite research to prove this point. It is obvious from ethnic jokes. While a joke about any other ethnic or religious group runs a greater risk of insensitivity and thus of disapproval, jokes about WASPs are always welcome and innocent. The assumed difference between WASPs and the other butts of ethnic jokes is that WASPs don't care—they are powerful, secure, above it all, out of reach of the malice.

What is a WASP's idea of a seven-course banquet? Answer: six Martinis and a Bremner Wafer. How many WASPs does it take to change a light bulb? Answer: two—one to call the electrician and one to mix the Martinis.

A WASP couple, Richard and Joan Maple, could be seen drinking Martinis in the 1979 movie *Too Far to Go* on NBC television. This was an upscale soap opera based on a collection of short stories by John Updike.[3] The significance of the Martini was not lost upon the reviewer in the *New York Times:* "The Maples are surrounded with the trappings of upper-middle-class Americana. . . . Martinis and needlepoint, yoga exercises and summer seaside homes are mixed judiciously with Steinberg posters and French movies on television and cognac."[4] Likewise, the Martini drinkers who populate the fictional suburb, Shady Hill, of John Cheever's short stories of the 1950s are WASPs. The fact that they drink Martinis is one of the things that makes them WASPs, and the fact that they are WASPs makes them drink Martinis. In a 1981 poem about "the last WASPs," Frederick Seidel writes:

> A fireside frost bloomed on the silver martini
> Shaker the magic evenings they could be home.[5]

Seidel, who is not much in sympathy with this vanishing generation, knows a lot about its mores, which include its indispensable drink.

Donald Barthelme used the WASP-Martini connection to good advantage in "The Teachings of Don B.: A Yankee Way of Knowledge."[6] It is a parody of Carlos Castaneda's *The Teachings of Don Juan: A Yaqui Way of Knowledge* (1968), a book that spoke to a generation—the hippies, dropouts, and counterculture elements of the 1960s. It was a purportedly true account of the encounter of Castaneda, a graduate student in anthropology, with the Mexican Indian shaman Don Juan. Though Don Juan's rhetoric was powerful, it was mushroom-induced trances that ultimately facilitated young Castaneda's initiation into the shamanic parallel universe. In the parody, the narrator, Xavier, goes, in 1966, to Don B. in Greenwich Village to learn "the secrets of certain hallucinogenic substances peculiar to Yankee culture." He is rebuffed, returns in 1968, and becomes Don B.'s apprentice. Finally Don B. agrees to "prepare the heart" of Xavier with a "yellow warmth," an expression that proves to refer to the twist of a lemon in a Martini on the rocks, though in keeping with the humor, neither the drink nor the ingredients are ever named. Xavier speaks of two vessels of colorless liquid, a yellow object, a knife, two glasses, and "six small colorless objects, each perhaps an inch and one-half square."

The Martini is drunk by patricians like Dr. Peter Knapp; it is a WASP drink; it is a "Yankee way of knowledge." In short, it is a marker of social class. Even if it is impossible to define "class" to the satisfaction of social scientists, the fact remains that people think that class exists, and they think that the Martini is upper-class. One of the illustrations in Paul Fussell's *Class* presents three arrays of magazines corresponding to the tastes of three classes of the several that he distinguishes. These are the upper-middle, the middle, and the "prole." Their names appear in the illustration next to their chosen reading material, but in order to make the classes instantly identifiable, the illustrator has added beverages. With the prole's *TV Guide* and *National Enquirer*, a can of Budweiser. With the upper-middle-class financial magazines, a Martini glass.[7]

When the rough-hewn Brian Kelly of the novel *The Naked Martini* (1964) went to Harvard, "he paid more attention to his fingernails, and let his crew cut grow out, and learned to mix a mean martini." The Martini is a bridge to the patrician world of Elizabeth Kirkland, whom he impresses with his mixological skill. Brian, of Irish immigrant stock, who had been told by his brother, "We come out of nowhere. We belong to nothing," thinks of himself as a "man-child, boy-dreamer and social climber." His upward trajectory carries him to Stamford, Connecticut. When Liz returns from her year abroad, Brian is "invited for the weekend to the great rambling Stamford house, a place of low porches drooping over the Sound, scraggly rose gardens and tall hedges and charcoal-faced servants who spilled Martinis out of silver-penguin pitchers." The Martini is so identified in Brian's mind with this upper-class milieu that he even uses "Martini" as a sort of code word when he greets Liz's mother: "'I'm fine, ma'am,' he said. 'I've been anticipating one of your martinis all the way up from New York.'" Left by himself for a moment, Brian recalls a party given here the previous summer:

> He remembered the slow smiles that broke upon their faces, mockery with an arrow in its side; heart-shaped faces as beautiful and bored as only the faces of the daughters of the rich can be. He remembered . . . cats on leashes, and olives impaled on pink toothpicks falling like pieces of the summer sky; and, of course, martinis, and smoked grass-hoppers *en brochette* and conversation like the scratch of chalk on a blackboard.[8]

The Martini is a high-status drink

Of course, Martinis. These are the sine qua non of upper-class existence. (Pink toothpicks and cats on leashes? I think that Fussell might rank these people a couple of notches below upper-class. But in the novel it is a matter of Brian's perception, not of reality.)

Brian wants to live in the household of an "Honora" (see "Historical Background of the Ambiguities"), to inhabit the world long since carved out for the Martini by advertising and by the attitudes that advertising partly created and partly reflected. This world is imaged most precisely in a Heublein advertisement from the turn of the century. A fashionable matron alights from her carriage and says to her butler, who is waiting at the door, "Before you do another thing, James, bring me a CLUB COCK-TAIL. I'm so tired of shopping. Make it a MARTINI" (Figure 1).

The upper-classness of this advertisement is so blatant that one suspects that the Martini, and thus the purveyors of bottled Martinis, had something to prove. In fact, as the descendant of the rough-and-tumble Gin Cocktail, the Martini in its earlier days did not immediately gain the allegiance of the class to which it aspired to belong. In Willa Cather's *A Lost Lady*, published in 1923 but set in a time "thirty or forty years ago" (i.e., the 1880s or 1890s), the smart set in the western town Sweet Water drink whiskey cocktails. The author explains, "Nobody drank Martinis then; gin was supposed to be the consolation of sailors and inebriate scrub-women."[9] These westerners will soon, however, realize that in the form of the Martini, gin has become respectable. The elegant new cocktail removes gin once and for all from its eighteenth-century depravity, which was held up to the world in William Hogarth's engraving *Gin Lane* (1750–51).[10]

By the end of the first decade of the twentieth century, the Martini had acquired the upper-status identity that it still has. The evidence on which I am relying consists of ten passages, mostly in prose fiction, published or written in 1910 or earlier.[11] They divide up much as do the seats on airplanes: first class, business, and tourist. Six are quite distinctly upper-class Martinis; three are the hard-driving businessman's Martini; and one is lower-class but with indications that the drink may already, even in this context, have had upper-class connotations. There is another, an eleventh passage that lies outside the category of class, associating the Martini with New York theater-going sophisticates.[12] (Sophisticated and upper-class are not the same thing. Both characteristics may occur in the same person, but they very often occur separately.)

The fictional businessmen are Jack London's Burning Daylight, who will appear in Ambiguity 1; David Graham Phillips's Ed Gideon, whom we shall meet in the next Simple Message; and Perkins. The last-named enters Martini history thanks to the bandleader and composer John Philip Sousa (1854–1932), who published a novel, *The Fifth String*, in 1902. It is

« FIGURE I »
A page from a Heublein brochure, ca. 1900. The Martini
is a high-status drink.
Photograph courtesy of Heublein, Inc.

about Angelo Diotti, an Italian violinist who comes to the United States
on a concert tour and falls in love with Mildred Wallace, the daughter
of a New York banker. The Martini appears early on, after Diotti's initial
success in New York. His manager, Perkins, goes to see him the next
morning:

> Perkins was happy—Perkins was positively joyous, and Perkins was self-
> satisfied. The violinist had made a great hit. But Perkins, confiding in the
> white-coated dispenser who concocted his *matin Martini,* very dry, an
> hour before, said he regarded the success due as much to the manage-
> ment as to the artist. And Perkins believed it. Perkins usually took all the
> credit for a success, and with charming consistency placed all responsi-
> bility for failure on the shoulders of the hapless artist.[13]

The Martini is a high-status drink

Here and in his only other appearance in the novella Perkins is characterized as bluff and materialistic, in refinement a cut below the other characters.

As for the upper-classness of the drink, the earliest known literary reference to the Martini, in a short story of 1896, makes it clear enough: "One of the *jeunesse dorée* in the party tipped his chair back as indication that he had retired from the argument, and as he sipped his Martini and inhaled its seductive bouquet, a far-away look came into his baby-blue eyes."[14] The Martini had arrived socially, overcoming the bad associations of gin, and was to be enshrined in the 1906 edition of *Mrs. Beeton's Book of Household Management,* where it was listed under the heading "American Drinks."[15] Further, the drink meant the same thing everywhere in the United States. In Philadelphia, on November 22, 1899, at a dinner for the judges of that city's dog show, the first course of Blue Point oysters was accompanied by Martinis.[16] In O. Henry's *The Gentle Grafter* (1904), the narrator, Parlez-vous Pickens, the gentle con artist of the title, and his partner, Caligula Polk, kidnap Colonel Jackson T. Rockingham, the mayor of Mountain Valley, Georgia. In order to serve him in the style to which they imagine he is accustomed, they invest $250 in fancy groceries. The first lunch: "So at twelve o'clock we had a hot lunch ready that looked like a banquet on a Mississippi River steamboat. We spread it on the tops of two or three big boxes, opened two quarts of the red wine, set the olives and a canned oyster cocktail and a ready-made Martini by the colonel's plate, and called him to grub."[17]

In the same decade Harvard men are drinking Martinis in Chicago. In 1910, in a story by Brand Whitlock about ward politics, Underwood, a well-born Chicagoan, Harvard graduate, lawyer, and aspiring politician, goes to pay his respects to Malachi Nolan, a saloon keeper and a boss in the Chicago ward in which Underwood is campaigning: "Underwood watched Malachi Nolan mix his [Underwood's] Martini cocktail, splash it picturesquely into a sparkling glass and bejewel it with a Maraschino cherry, then gravely take a cigar for himself and stow it away in his ample waistcoat. Then, as Nolan mopped the bar with a professional sweep of his white-sleeved, muscular arm. . . ."[18] The maraschino cherry, by the way, is not an aberration; it was quite common in the sweet Martini of yesteryear. In G. H. Lorimer's novel of 1906, Jack Spurlock, who has been expelled from Harvard, also drinks a Martini in Chicago in the first decade of this century. His father has required him to take a job in the Chicago branch of the family firm. Jack describes himself on the way to work on the first morning: "I stopped the cab and sopped up a dry Martini."[19] He should be the businessman that his father is, and the drink ought to be the businessman's Martini, but at the moment, his Martini is just the privilege of his class.

In the decade under discussion, the only textual reference to a Martini drunk by lower-class persons suggests that they have to be deceived into drinking it. The reference is in *The Mixer and Server*, the journal of the Hotel and Restaurant Employes' International Alliance and Bartenders' International League of America.[20] This journal regularly published short articles and excerpts from other publications. In 1901 it published, from something called "Exchange," an article called "'Joe Smith Cocktail.'" The title of the article appears in quotation marks, which are designed to put the reader on guard. The article begins, "'No, it isn't a Martini, just a straight cocktail,' said Mr. Joseph Smith, as he handed one out to a patron." It emerges that Smith is a bartender in an establishment on the east side of Faneuil Hall in Boston, and that his new cocktail has made him the cynosure of the "marketmen" (i.e., the men who work in the meat market there). The joke comes in the next-to-last paragraph, where Smith gives his recipe for the cocktail. It turns out to be a Martini.[21]

The marketmen like a Martini only as a Joe Smith Cocktail. Their instinct is good. They already know that it is someone else's drink, and history will bear them out. Dr. Peter Knapp and his ilk will be the Martini-drinkers of the world.

The Martini is a high-status drink

The Martini is a man's, not a woman's, drink

I made him a third martini, but the women came and made us eat something, which spoiled a very promising evening.—RUSSELL BAKER, 1979

THE MALENESS of the Martini is reflected in two beliefs: first, that women cannot mix Martinis; second, that women, given a choice, do not drink Martinis. Both of these beliefs are, of course, mistaken, and bear no relation to reality. But symbolism, not reality, is my subject.

The first belief is obviously in contradiction to the conjugal Martini that the wife mixes for her husband upon his return from work or, as the case may be, from loafing. At the opening of *Shadow of the Thin Man* (1941), Nick is in the park with his son, sitting on a bench and reading the racing form. Cut to Nora in their suite in the St. Cloud Hotel. She wonders where he is; looks into the park through binoculars; sees him and Nick Jr. sitting on the bench. She then vigorously shakes a shiny metal cocktail shaker. Cut to Nick in the park. He perks up in reaction to an invisible signal. "Nicky," he says to his son, "something tells me that something important is happening somewhere and I think we should be there." The maid Stella, watching through the binoculars, is astounded to see Nick get up and start toward the hotel. She asks Nora if he could hear the shaker or smell the drink. Nora's explanation: "This is a cocktail." When he arrives, the Martini is waiting for him on a table near the door. He gulps it down (in one of the violations of Martini manners in which the Thin Man films abound).

But in the same decade as the film, Bernard DeVoto had to write,

"There is a widespread notion that women cannot make martinis, just as some islanders believe that they cast an evil spell on the tribal fishnets. This is a vagrant item of male egotism: the art of the martini is not a sex-linked character."[1] DeVoto's egalitarian view of the Martini—the one embodied in the conjugal Martini and clearly illustrated for millions in *Shadow of the Thin Man*—and the sexist one continued to exist side by side. In 1965, sixteen years after DeVoto wrote, a Beefeater advertising brochure gave this advice:

> Let the head of the house assume the responsibility for the martini. You can, of course, get someone else to do it—a paid hand on a yacht, a but-ler if you possess one.
>
> But don't ask a wife to put the pitcher and the glasses in the refrigera-tor, or to preside over the swift chilly marriage of gin and vermouth. She has probably been in and out of the kitchen all day on lesser errands.

Robert Donohoe tactfully stated this point of view in 1997 when, in re-sponse to my question on the matter, he said, "I have never seen a woman mix a Martini," meaning with the exception of women bartenders.[2]

In 1978, Beefeater brought out a full-page advertisement based on the second belief, that women, given a choice, do not drink Martinis. The page is divided into halves crosswise. The top half shows a woman's and a man's face, each with a glass just below the lips, and a suggestion of the left index finger. In the bottom half of the page a caption is embla-zoned beneath each face. Beneath the woman's it reads, "I like to give my gin and tonic the same advantage he gives his martini."[3]

As the dominant one will drink a Martini and the other something else when two men are drinking together (see Simple Message 6), so—all the more so—will a woman drink something weaker than a Martini when she is drinking with a man. Unless, of course, it is the Martini-of-the-relationship, to which I shall return later.

Susan Lenox, a character created by David Graham Phillips, provides, at different times in her life, an example of each of the woman's two strategies: choose something weaker; drink the Martini with the man. She was born 1879, out of wedlock. Her mother died in childbirth. She was raised by her aunt in a prosperous household in a small town in Ohio. At age seventeen, through a series of misunderstandings, she came under suspicion of having lost her virginity. Fearing that his family would be disgraced, her once loving uncle arranged an instant marriage for her with his brother's uncouth farmhand. After two nights Susan ran away and lived in Cincinnati, where she drifted into prostitution, an outcome presented by Phillips as all but inevitable. His muckraking novel is *Susan Lenox: Her Fall and Rise* (written before 1911 and thus a valuable source for the early development of Martini symbolism).[4] In its 964 pages, Susan goes back and forth between prostitution and doomed attempts to live a respectable life.

In New York she takes a job as a model with a dress manufacturer. On the first day of work, however, she is compelled to accept a dinner invitation from a potential client of her company, Ed Gideon from Chicago. He is "a fifteen-thousand-a-year man on the way to a partnership." He offers her a cocktail; she chooses sherry. He orders a dry Martini for himself, then a second, which he finishes before she finishes her sherry. (The year is about 1898, the same year in which another hard-driving businessman, Burning Daylight, becomes a Martini drinker in San Francisco; see Ambiguity 1.) She spends the night with him, in order to secure the big order that he promises to place with her company, but quits her job in disgust the next day and tries once more to find honest work.[5] In this episode the Martini is "his," as in the Beefeater advertisement. He has money and power. He is going to possess her in spite of her reluctance, which Phillips is at pains to describe. Her drink—sherry—signals, in contrast to the Martini, her subordinate position. If one were to state the matter in terms of the Martini itself, then, as wife says to husband in a New Yorker cartoon of 1986, "I'm supposed to be sort of the vermouth in this marriage, right?"[6]

If the martini is "his" by definition, it is easy to see why there is a Martini-of-the-relationship. Because the Martini is not the woman's, her participation in the drinking of a Martini is a submission to the maleness of the drink, a symbolic submission to the man.[7] Consider this exchange between Hemingway's Colonel Cantwell and Renata in Harry's Bar in Venice (we shall find them again in Ambiguity 2):

> "Then let us have another Martini," the girl said. "You know I never drank a Martini until we met."
> "I know. But you drink them awfully well."[8]

The drinking of the first Martini almost stands for loss of virginity. But the colonel compensates her for the loss by paying her the greatest compliment of which he is capable. The greatest compliment that a man can pay a woman is to say that she drinks the Martini well, that she *is his equal* in the Martini-of-the-relationship.

Or the woman can use the Martini to her own advantage. At a certain point, reduced to the depths of poverty and despair, Susan Lenox returns to prostitution, this time, however, with a resolve. She moves out of her tawdry room with only a few dollars and the clothes on her back. At Broadway and Twenty-eighth, a man called Brent offers her a drink. She accepts. They go to a cafe that has an adjoining restaurant. He asks:

"What are you drinking?"

"What are *you* drinking?" asked Susan, still covertly watching Brent.

"You are going to dine with me?"

"I've no engagement."

"Then let's have Martinis—and I'll go get a table and order dinner while the waiter's bringing them."[9]

If it is going to be a before-dinner drink, then the Martini is the choice (in preference to what, we do not know). But the Martini has a further significance here: a woman's drinking a Martini with a man is an act of acquiescence, and Brent will take it as such. But this time it is a deliberate and chosen acquiescence, not an enforced one. Consider Susan's reflections in the interim of Brent's absence. None of the women she sees around her in this "triumphant class" of persons would be there without the assistance of a man. "The successful women won their success by disposing of their persons to advantage—by getting the favor of some man of ability. . . . She must make the best bargain she could. . . . There was no other way open to her. . . . Other ways there might be—for other women. But not for her, the outcast." She moves on to a life of steady prostitution. Her choice of this life was signaled in her question, "What are *you* drinking?" The answer is the male Martini. To drink it is to dispose of herself to her advantage, which is merely sexual, the only advantage left to her.

The maleness of the drink can even be a substitute for potency. In Hemingway's *The Sun Also Rises* (1926), the hero, Jake, who is impotent because of a war wound, has a relationship, albeit sexually manqué, with Lady Brett. He goes to Madrid to comfort her after she has broken up with her latest boyfriend, and in the penultimate scene of the novel they drink Martinis together. The drink seems to replace the consummation with which the novel would have ended happily:

> We sat on high stools at the bar while the barman shook martinis in a large nickelled shaker. . . . We touched the two glasses as they stood side by side on the bar. They were coldly beaded. Outside the curtained window was the summer heat of Madrid.
>
> "I like an olive in a Martini," I said to the barman.
>
> "Right you are, sir. There you are."
>
> "Thanks."
>
> "I should have asked, you know."[10]

The absence of the olive, of the seed-bearing ovoid fruit, seems to stand for Jake's condition, and in fact I have heard the Martini without olive referred to as "castrated." The plight of Lady Brett and Jake is thus transposed into the Martini itself. And yet the defect in the Martini can be repaired, and the drink can excel and replace the unfulfilled relationship.

To return, in conclusion, to the world as it is, women do, of course, drink Martinis. They drink them with one another and also alone. A woman, M. F. K. Fisher, has made the finest statement on the loner's Martini (quoted in Ambiguity 1). The coincidence by which her article on the Martini appeared in the same year, 1949, as DeVoto's in *Harper's*, is significant, and so is the fact that hers preceded his by eleven months.[11] Even in those days, appreciation of the Martini was a woman's as much as a man's province.

The Martini is optimistic,
not pessimistic

Then I remembered our standing at the bar having a Martini, and I had the won-derful inner feeling of relief that comes when you have bet yourself out of a bad hole and I was wondering how badly the bet had hit him. — ERNEST HEMING-WAY, 1938

THE WORKING DAY contains two major turning points, at which pain, worry, fatigue, and depression give way to their opposites and optimism is reborn, with the Martini's help.

One of the turning points is lunch. Jimmy Carter's denunciation of the "three-Martini lunch" brought forth hundreds of letters to newspa-pers in defense of this institution, and it is a pity that an anthology of these letters has not been published, since they express with such feel-ing, and sometimes with eloquence, all of the Simple Messages of the Martini. The message of optimism appears in a letter from Mr. John H. Keppler of Lawrence, Long Island, apparently a retired businessman, to the *New York Times*. The "three-Martini lunch," he says, "produced an ambience of buoyant vigor and well-being in which far-reaching plans and sound judgments were made about the future condition of man."[1]

The other turning point in the day is the cocktail hour, of which DeVoto wrote in 1951, "It marks the lifeward turn. The heart wakens from coma and its dyspnea ends. Its strengthening pulse is to cross over into the campground, to believe that the world has not been altogether lost or, if lost, not altogether in vain."[2] He concludes his essay with the fol-lowing advice on the Martini-rite: "Tranquillity ought normally to come

"*It was a very bleak period in my life, Louie. Martinis didn't help. Religion didn't help. Psychiatry didn't help. Transcendental meditation didn't help. Yoga didn't help. But Martinis helped a little.*"

« FIGURE 2 »
The Martini as the drink of hope
Henry Martin © 1975 from The New Yorker Collection.

with sight of the familiar bottles. If it doesn't, feel free to hum some simple tune as you go about your preparations. . . . Do not whistle, for your companions are sinking into the quiet of expectation. And you need not sing, for presently there will be singing in your heart."[3] One is reborn in the Martini.

The Martini can also bring about or mark a change in the mood of longer periods in one's life. The Martini has this function at the end of a story by F. Scott Fitzgerald called "The Rich Boy." This is the story, by the way, in which Fitzgerald said, "Let me tell you about the very rich. They are different from you and me." The rich boy is Anson Hunter. He inherits money, makes money, lives high, and is a big drinker, but he is also a Sunday school teacher, a moral adviser to family and friends, and hardworking to a fault. At the end of the story, when he is on the verge of collapse, the older members of his brokerage firm send him on a vacation to Europe. The narrator of the story is traveling on the same boat, and in the final scene they have a drink together: "We walked into the bar with that defiant feeling that characterizes the day of departure and ordered four Martinis [i.e., two apiece]. After one cocktail a change came over him—he suddenly reached across and slapped my knee with the first joviality I had seen him exhibit for months."[4] With the Martini, Anson, who is only thirty but had lapsed into "intense nervousness" and "the fussy pessimism of a man of forty," regains his youth and optimism. The Martini is, as Cole Porter's two little babes in the woods discovered, the fountain of youth.

Tom Lehrer gave voice to the same notion in 1959 in "Bright College Days," a parody of the Old School Song. It can be heard on a record called *An Evening Wasted with Tom Lehrer.* The song ends:

> Hearts full of youth, hearts full of truth,
> Six parts gin to one part vermouth.[5]

The Martini is the fountain of youth and the water of life, and, as such, it is the pivot on which the moods of the day, or of longer periods, turn.

A final and somewhat complex example of this optimistic Martini occurs in the song by Frank Loesser, "I Believe in You," sung by a young executive to himself in the musical *How to Succeed in Business without Really Trying* (1962). The song contains three stanzas. In the first, the "you" of the title is identified primarily as young. In the second, he is compared with a tiger, and in the third, with a Martini:

> You have the cool, clear eyes of a seeker of wisdom and truth,
> Yet there's the slam bang tang reminiscent of gin and vermouth.

(Truth and vermouth seem to cry out for each other.) The point of the young man's comparison of himself with a Martini is that he is full of promise. It happens that Loesser was writing within a year or two of W. H. Auden's 1963–64 haiku on the Martini, which will be discussed apropos of Ambiguity 4. Auden used the tiger as a standard by which the toughness of the Martini-drinker could be measured. In Auden, one found the equation tiger, Martini, survival (i.e., toughness). In Loesser, it is tiger, Martini, youth. Structurally, the song and the haiku are identical, if toughness and youth are taken as complementary. The analysis and comparison of Loesser and Auden show once again that the Martini's associations belong to a system, one that can even produce surprisingly detailed replications of the sort just witnessed.

The comparison of Loesser and Auden is also the comparison of a simple message (the Martini is optimistic) and the negative side of an ambiguity (the Martini is tough). Auden expresses a pessimistic humanism: we have the toughness to survive, and the Martinis that we wretches drink prove it. Loesser, as befits the genre in which he is working, tells us that our faith can be renewed, we can cross over to the campground with DeVoto, and the "tang" of the Martini helps.

The Martini is the drink of adults, not of children

Now run and play, pussy. Mommy's going up to the hotel and have a Martini with Mrs. Hubbel. I'll bring you the olive.—J. D. SALINGER, 1948

PLAYING ON Franklin Roosevelt's expression "the children's hour" (see "Historical Background of the Ambiguities"), Beefeater Gin advertised itself—in the form, of course, of a Martini—as the drink of "the grown-ups' hour." A brochure of the 1970s advised, "Summon the children just before you mix the martini. Announce to them that it is now the *grown-ups'* hour—and they are to pursue their play elsewhere. The martini hour is for those who are going to drink martinis." In this way children will learn that the Martini is the drink of adulthood. To be an adult is to drink Martinis.

The six-year-old heroine of *Eloise,* a popular children's book of 1955, lives in the Plaza with her English nanny and her dog, Weenie. Eloise's mother never appears in the book, and her father is never mentioned. Except for her nanny and the personnel of the Plaza, adults do not fig-ure in Eloise's experience. But she does know something about them: "Sometimes my mother goes to Virginia with her lawyer. . . . Here's what he likes: Martinis."[1] The book has a drawing of the lawyer, Martini in hand.

To drink Martinis is to become an adult. The Owl Club at Harvard, an undergraduate fraternal organization, inducts its new members through a "Martini ritual." In a public room of the club the initiate must consume several Martinis in rapid succession. He is then led blindfolded on hands and knees through an obstacle course into the private rooms, to which only members have access. The Martini is part of a trial, a *rite de passage,* by which the new member becomes a fellow club*man.*[2]

At the opposite end of the social scale from the members of the Owl Club, in *An American Tragedy* (1925), Clyde Griffiths's fellow bellhops in Kansas City frequent a restaurant that they consider upscale, although in fact it is "little more than an excellent chophouse," says Theodore Dreiser. "Eating here, they somehow felt older, wiser, and more important—real men of the world." Clyde accompanies them to one of their monthly dinners. They order cocktails in a self-conscious fashion, each choosing something different. The Martini-drinker is Arthur Kinsella. "In a sort of ostentatious way, he drew back his coat sleeves, seized a bill of fare, and scanning the drink-list on the back, exclaimed: 'Well, a dry Martini is good enough for a start.'" Though Clyde himself does not drink a Martini, the dinner is the first step on his road to perdition, to the "American tragedy" of the novel's title. His sexual initiation takes place at a bordello later that evening. His life as an adult is beginning. As he reflects when he decides to go to the dinner, "He was not to be held back by any suggestion which his mother [an evangelist] could now make."[3]

The Martini conferred adulthood on Truman Capote at a cocktail party given by Carmel Snow, senior editor of *Harper's Bazaar,* in 1945 or 1946. Diminutive of stature and cherubic of face, he looked like a child, though he was in his early twenties, and Snow handed him a glass of milk. Informed by her fiction editor that he was the author of short stories published in her magazine and in its rival, *Mademoiselle,* she quickly replaced the milk with a Martini.[4]

Since the Martini separates children from adults, it is shocking or funny to find a child mixing Martinis. In "The Fall of Edward Barnard," the Maugham story cited earlier (Simple Message 1), it is shocking, at least to Bateman Hunter. In the novel *Auntie Mame,* it is funny. Here is the author's brief description of ten-year-old Patrick's first summer at Beekman Place: "My advancement that summer of 1929, if not exactly what *Every Parent's Magazine* would recommend, was remarkable. By the end of *July* I knew how to mix what Mr. Woollcott called a 'Lucullan little martini' and I had learned not to be frightened by Auntie Mame's most astonishing friends."[5]

These sentences were expanded into the Martini-mixing scene in the play (1957) and the musical (1967). Mr. Babcock, Auntie Mame's lawyer, comes to the apartment and is received by Patrick. While they wait for Auntie Mame, Patrick offers Mr. Babcock a Martini and, to Babcock's astonishment, mixes it for him. The stage directions provide for an "in-and-out" Martini, although this term is not used. This Martini is, of course, an anachronism in the 1920s, but it hardly matters. Patrick "uncorks the vermouth, pours a smidgeon into a glass, sloshes it around, then empties it completely." He then pours the iced gin into the glass, adds a twist of lemon, and serves the astonished Babcock. At this moment Auntie Mame appears and says, "I wonder if it makes the best first impression on a sensitive young mind to see you drinking during business hours."[6] The real lesson is, however, the one that Patrick has already learned from Auntie Mame: the Martini is what sets adults apart from children.[7] Patrick's ability to mix a Martini only sets him, comically, apart from other children.

To offer a child a Martini would be the most flagrant kind of boundary-crossing. In Roald Dahl's story "Georgy Porgy" (1959), a country curate, age thirty-one, recalls his mother:

> And in the evening she used to sit on the sofa in her black trousers with her feet tucked up underneath her, smoking endless cigarettes from a long black holder. And I'd be crouching on the floor, watching her.
> "You want to taste my martini, George?" she used to ask.
> "Now stop it, Clare," my father would say. "If you're not careful you'll stunt the boy's growth."
> "Go on," she said. "Don't be frightened of it. Drink it."
> I always did everything my mother told me.
> "That's enough," my father said. "He only has to know what it tastes like."[8]

The Martini is only the first example of the mother's extreme eccentricity, which leaves the adult George a sexual neurotic.

J. D. Salinger, the author of fiction for adults about children and adolescents, avails himself of the Martini as a marker of age group. After Holden Caulfield flunks out of Pencey Prep, the third prep school that he has attended, he returns to Manhattan and holes up in a seedy hotel, afraid to return to his parents' home. *The Catcher in the Rye* now becomes a series of misadventures that deepen Holden's alienation. He reaches out for companionship to Luce, who had been his student adviser at Whooton. They meet in the bar of a swanky hotel. Holden is drinking Scotch and soda, bent on getting drunk. Luce orders a very dry Martini, with no olive and, exasperated by Holden's questions about sex, articulates the central question of the novel: "When are you going to grow up?" Luce has a second Martini and asks the bartender to "make it a lot dryer." Though in terms of alcoholic strength the Martini and the Scotch and soda may be equal, the Martini designates the dominant member of the pair of drinkers (as in the case of James Bond and Leiter, described in Ambiguity 4). As shown by his precise instructions to the bartender, Luce knows what he is doing, and he is in control of himself. He leaves after two drinks; Holden stays on and proceeds to get drunk.[9]

Franny and her friend Lane Coutell, college students, are exerting

The Martini is the drink of adults

themselves to be grown up in Salinger's story "Franny." Franny arrives at Lane's college for the weekend. They proceed to lunch at a restaurant the specialty of which is frogs' legs. They order Martinis. He is a pompous undergraduate intellectual and a monopolizer of conversation. Her defense is to reply to his rantings about Flaubert with comments about the Martini: "She sipped her Martini. 'This is marvellous,' she said, looking at the glass. 'I'm so glad it's not about twenty to one. I hate it when they're absolutely all gin.'" Lane continues to orate on Flaubert, demanding assent rather than discussion: "Know what I mean?" She replies, "You going to eat your olive, or what?" Then she realizes that she did not really want the olive. "There was nothing to do, though, when Lane extended his Martini glass to her but to accept the olive and consume it with apparent relish." The awkwardness continues to build. She detests the intellectual style that he is trying to achieve. Her own preoccupation is a certain technique of meditation that she has discovered. She passes out during lunch, and the weekend is effectively over. Two intelligent, attractive young persons have failed to make human contact. The Martini, which, like the frogs' legs and the intellectualism, should have shown that they were adults, showed that they were still children.[10]

The Martini belongs to the past,
not to the present

There's prandial Perrier, the executive swig,
Now that lunchtime Martinis are infra dig. — FRANK ZACHARY, 1979

THE MARTINI EVOKES an image of some past decade—the 1920s, the
1930s, the 1940s, the 1950s, or even the 1960s, depending on your point
of view.[1] Writing about furniture in the style of Syrie Maugham, who set
the decorating fashion of the 1920s and 1930s, Joan Kron began, "You can
almost hear the ice cubes tinkling in the martini shakers, the backgam-
mon chips clacking and Noel Coward making witty remarks as you
pass Stuart Greet's new shop at 783 Madison Avenue near 68th street."[2]
These were the images conjured up by the Syrie Maugham furniture in
the shop window.

Is the Martini in fact a drink of the past? At the end of the 1970s, it
was. Michael Korda wrote in 1977, "The martini is seldom seen among
those who have serious business to discuss and has long since been
replaced by the glass of white wine, the spritzer (wine and soda) and Perrier water with a slice of lime."[3] Statistics published by *Forbes* bore him
out.[4] *Forbes* sent reporters to four well-known expense-account restaurants. The Four Seasons in New York served a total of 373 alcoholic drinks
at lunch on October 12, 1977. Of these, a mere five were Martinis, and
for each Martini, forty-seven glasses of wine were served. On October
13 at the Cantina D'Italia in Washington, D.C., guests ordered one hundred drinks, of which nine were Martinis, and the ratio of wine to Martinis was eleven to one. In Houston, again on October 12, the Martini
was in only slightly greater demand: 20 out of a total of 385 drinks at

Maxim. On October 12 in Los Angeles, Scandia's customers consumed 370 drinks, 9 of them Martinis. One of three drinks was wine. The relation of wine to the Martini was now, it seemed, the opposite of what it had been in the late 1920s, a period of which Sarah Bradford wrote, "The shadow of the dry martini . . . lay across the wine trade."[5] Wine was now in the sun and cast a shadow on the Martini.

How much had the Martini declined? In 1964 the *New Yorker* interviewed Fernand Petiot, head bartender at the St. Regis for thirty years: "According to M. Petiot, . . . the mixed drink most popular at the hotel is the Martini. 'We serve from two hundred to three hundred a day,' he said."[6] In 1978 I talked on the telephone to John Xenos, then the head bartender, and was told that the St. Regis Bar, the King Cole Bar, and room service then served a total of about 125 Martinis a day. M. Petiot had probably been talking about the St. Regis Bar alone. One could venture, then, to say that the Martini's popularity at the St. Regis had declined by about 66 percent since 1964.

Roughly the same was true of L'Omelette in Palo Alto, California. This restaurant handed out numbered postcards with its Martinis until 1970. I once had in my possession the card that came with Martini 3,023,924, and it was dated November 23, 1962. Since L'Omelette opened in 1932, it must have been serving Martinis at the rate of 100,771 a year, assuming a steady rate of yearly consumption. That would mean about 270 a day, up through 1962. In 1978 I called L'Omelette and was told that they then served about one hundred a day. The percentage of decline was thus about the same as at the St. Regis.

What was the surviving Martini like? From John Xenos, from L'Omelette, from bartenders in Boston, and from innumerable conversations on the subject, I concluded that vodka Martinis outnumbered gin Martinis by at least three to two and probably by five to one—not surprising, when one considers that vodka outsold gin by thirteen million cases in 1977.[7] At most 20 percent and probably as few as 5 percent of all Martinis were served straight up. In other words, the Martini of the late 1970s was vodka on the rocks.[8]

For the revised edition of this book, I did not continue this kind of research. L'Omelette is now a Walgreens drugstore. In any case, the research would not have been easy to continue, given the great variety of drinks going under the name "Martini." An even better reason for my neglect of statistics has already appeared in the introduction: the Martini is always of the past, no matter how many Martinis, of whatever recipe, are being drunk at any particular time. What is of interest in this book is the image of the Martini, and the past belongs to its image.

In the introduction I distinguished between two visions of the past that the Martini conjures up in the 1990s. One, in the retro style, is the

1940s and 1950s. The other is a personal past, extending from one's own lifetime back into one's father's generation, and thence in an unbroken line to all the previous generations of Martini-drinkers. Typically, those for whom the Martini expresses a personal past believe that the Martini is coming to end with them, just as WASPs are always believed, both by non-WASPs and by members of the species, to be the "last WASPs" (cf. Frederick Seidel in Simple Message 3). Robert Donohoe, quoted in the introduction, is a spokesman of this doomsday view for the 1990s. It was also stated eloquently by Donald G. Smith in 1985:

> The demise of the martini is a sad thing and I hate to see it end with my generation. Not only is a grand old tradition dying, but our society is also losing something of nobility and character. The martini is an honest drink, tasting exactly like what it is and nothing else. There is no sugar in a martini; no egg whites, no black and white rums, no shaved almonds, no fruit juice, no chocolate, and no spices. A martini is not served in a pineapple shell nor a piece of rolled up canoe bark, and there are no disgusting pieces of flotsam around the top. It is a clear, clean, cold, pure, honest drink—especially designed for people with established values and a liking for purity, even in their vices.
>
> I regret the slow passing of this old friend from our culture, just as I regretted seeing the last Studebaker dealer and the end of single-wing football. I don't like knowing that there is something higher than the Empire State Building. Why do good things always have to pass away? Tonight I'm going to pour a martini and give this matter a lot of thought.[9]

Here the Martini is not only identified with the past; it is also the drink of a generation that had "established values." These probably include all the Simple Messages except optimism. Though Smith does not use the word "American," for him the Martini is associated with other images of an older America. With redeeming self-irony, Smith perfectly states the outlook of the traditionalist Martini-drinker, who sees in the demise of the drink the sign of a broader decline.

The demise of the Martini can also be an event in one's own life story, if one has had to stop drinking or to stop drinking this drink. An article by Loudon Wainwright in the *New York Times Magazine* in 1977 began:

> The stout man walked toward me along Sixth Avenue, his big face as red on that cold December day as if he'd fallen asleep on a beach in July. Blood pressure, I thought, wondering where my own was. Booze, I thought, too, calculating the number of drinks he might have had with lunch. Three or four, I figured, quite possibly martinis, my own mourned favorite. He looked, in his tweed jacket with his neck flaming out of the blue button-down collar, like men I remembered drinking and laughing with my father

on smoky Saturday afternoons at Princeton in the 1930s. They would all joke and playfully crunch great camel's hair shoulders into each other as we shuffled downhill along leaf-strewn sidewalks toward a football game.[10]

Wainwright constructs a complex comparison between himself and an unnamed stout man, who, he will go on to say, is a friend whom he has not seen for thirty years. (They walk past each other; the other man does not recognize Wainwright; no contact is made.) Wainwright has stopped drinking Martinis; the friend probably still drinks them. As a nondrinker of the Martini, Wainwright, by the principle embodied in Simple Message 6, goes, mentally, into a different generation from his friend, who reminds him of his father's friends. So the Martini is not only something in Wainwright's personal past but also the drink of his father's generation. (Other Simple Messages are, of course, at work here too—especially the third [upper status] and the fourth [man's drink], and one notes the mention of football, as in Smith's requiem.)

The Simple Messages Reconsidered

As said in the introduction, the binary oppositions on which the Simple Messages are based include a hierarchical ranking. The first term is good or superior, the second bad or inferior. If one converts the messages into a description of a person, one ends up with an adult American male who is urbane, upper-class, optimistic, and conservative ("conservative" is the translation of "of the past"). This person is superior; everyone else is inferior. As I have already suggested (Simple Messages 3 and 4), the businessman is the embodiment of this description (and Jack London's Burning Daylight will provide an example in Ambiguity 1). Referring to the Simple Messages as I had presented them in the first edition of this book, William Grimes appropriately commented:

> It could also be argued that the martini is capitalist. It is the official drink of America's business class, the high-octane fuel that powered Wall Street and Madison Avenue well into the 1970s, when the age of Perrier and lime began. A left-leaning social critic might propose that these professions, involving more than the usual compromises required by adult life, find their antidote in the martini, whose clarity and purity represent the uncorrupted soul of the corrupt man, just as the preppy look pays homage to youthful idealism and physical grace. In a world built on compromise, the businessman can insist with utter fanaticism on the martini as he likes it, *demands* it: drier than dry.[1]

The businessman is indeed one of the chief Martini-drinkers and regularly plays a role in cartoons, Martini jokes, and Martini-focused advertisements for gin.

35

But if the businessman is the embodiment of the Simple Messages, then one can see why no umbrage should be taken by anyone, child, woman, foreigner, or nonbusinessman. Not only is the Martini-drinking businessman open to irony and mockery, there is also the fact that the Martini as image is not exclusively his. The experience of the 1990s should have made that clear. The Martini is a highly complex and fungible image, and even as the American cocktail, which I would say is its primary or "default" message, it can express itself in a variety of ways. Max Rudin sees the Martini as epitomizing

> the essential American modernist style: powerful yet understated, with both guts and grace, tough yet elegant, spare and simple yet suggesting great complexity.
> . . . Combining energy and austerity, power and subtlety, urbanity and sophistication, all in a sexy, elegantly simple, streamlined package, the martini is the essence of American modernism in drinkable form. It's modern America as a cocktail.[2]

Rudin here brings out an aspect of the drink that was not much apparent in the Simple Messages, namely, its looks, its aesthetic appeal. With this aspect in mind, I could reformulate the approach outlined in my introduction and say that the thing, the drink itself, has a certain look—especially because of its characteristic glass—and the look is essential to, though not identical to, its image. (The image also has something to do with gin, with the customs that became associated with the drink, etc.)

I tried to isolate messages that were simple and unambiguous, but it does not take long to see how complex they really are. As an American drink, it is primarily used by Americans, the great *bricoleurs*, who are going to exploit its various symbolic possibilities for their own ends. The businessman may express his power by means of the Martini, but in a *New Yorker* cartoon it is the Martini that will be used to satirize him.[3] It works both ways. (This quality of American culture is the one most inaccessible to European intellectuals, who always take everything in the United States as serious, simple, and straightforward, and mistakenly assume that we do, too.)[4] Barnaby Conrad has presented an alternative vision of the Martini as expressing the very heterogeneity of the United States:

> One might see the Martini as an extended metaphor for Euro-American culture itself. Gin's history is Dutch and English—and from these countries came the dominant ethnic groups that settled North America, signed the Declaration of Independence, and created the greatest capitalist society in the world. Invented in Napoleonic times, French vermouth calls to

mind the Louisiana Purchase; indeed this beverage entered America through New Orleans. Italian vermouth's move from sweet to dry mirrors the Italian immigrant's assimilation. The lemon is the Caribbean or Latin American culture, while the olive is Italian or Greek, and the pickled onion is German or Jewish. The switch to vodka predates Perestroika and Glasnost but cannot be separated from America's Cold War fascination with Russian and Eastern European politics.[5]

It's a small point, but I would say that vodka was homeopathic medicine that Americans imbibed during the Cold War to harden themselves against the Soviet enemy. (And it worked!)

The Ambiguities
of the Martini

The Martini is civilized—
the Martini is uncivilized

T HE HERO of Hemingway's *A Farewell to Arms* (1929), Frederic Henry, defects from the Italian army, having concluded a "separate peace," and makes his way to Stresa to rejoin his lover, Catherine Barkley. He checks in at the Grand-Hôtel & des Îles Borromées and heads for the bar. There he drinks two Martinis, eats olives, salted almonds, and potato chips, and orders sandwiches. "The sandwiches came and I ate three and drank a couple more martinis. I had never tasted anything so cool and clean. They made me feel civilized."[1] As a new civilian, Frederic Henry celebrates with the drink of civilization. "Civilized" was the word that described the Martini in the burst of post-Prohibition advertising by liquor companies. A Martini and Rossi advertisement in *Vanity Fair* of March 1934 states, "They're disappearing fast, thank goodness—those vicious liquid heart-burns. People are going back to civilized cocktails—Martinis." In Dixie Belle Gin advertisements of this year, there begin to appear those Martini-drinking couples in evening clothes, those paragons of urbanity, who have continued to frequent the pages of gin advertising up to the present.

These couples are drinking one of the main kinds of civilized Martinis, the Martini-of-the-relationship. If we try, however, to imagine a life for them after the beautiful moment portrayed in the advertisement, they will be married. The husband will be drinking the Martini at a businessmen's lunch, or, as paterfamilias, he will be celebrating the Martini-rite at home. In short, the Martini that initiates or consecrates the relationship will give way to the other main kind of civilized Martini, the communal Martini. In this form, the drink plays a part in forming various groups of which society makes and remakes itself—a club, a cocktail party, the crowd at a bar, a family gathering, or a coterie. The Martini has even been served at church functions. It is in each case the totem-drink that binds together the members of the tribe. Accordingly, the mixing of the Martini is a rite, whether performed by the host or by the bartender, either of whom may assume the role of priest.

If the Martini is the source of such harmony, how can it be uncivilized, too? The answer was already implicit in the deprecation of the "three-Martini lunch." The Martini epitomizes excess. Therefore, it is the drink favored by those who take more than their just share. In Sinclair Lewis's *Babbitt* of 1922, the politician Jake Offutt says to the real estate agent Henry J. Thompson:

> Wonder how long we can keep it up, Hank? We're safe as long as the good little boys like George Babbitt . . . think you and me are rugged patriots. There's swell pickings for an honest politician here, Hank. A whole city to provide cigars and fried chicken and dry martinis for us. . . . Honest, Hank, a smart codger like me ought to be ashamed if he didn't milk cattle like them when they come around mooing for it![2]

In the midwestern city of Zenith in the early 1920s, the delicacy that Jake Offutt paired with the Martini was fried chicken. In 1966 a doctor and an author of self-improvement books wrote *Martinis and Whipped Cream: The New Carbo-Cal Way to Lose Weight and Stay Slim.* Martinis and whipped cream? To me these are opposites. One comes before a meal, the other, if at all, at the end. One is dry, the other sweet. But the authors thought of the two as complements, like bread and butter. Martinis and whipped cream were two of the delights enjoyed by the new dieters, who were "literally having an epicurean ball," now that they had stopped counting calories and begun to count only "carbo-cals."[3] The Martini, then, was a way of signifying the self-indulgence to which the book invited overweight persons.

Another explanation for the Martini's bad reputation lies, paradoxically, in the very refinement and elegance of this drink. The Martini is the civilized antidote to civilization, and therefore, like any antidote, it can become a poison if it is used in excess or for the wrong purposes, as, in popular belief, it is used by alcoholics. George L. Herter and Berthe E. Herter write, "An American martini is . . . just a drink for alcoholics who want a quick alcohol jolt regardless of taste."[4] The notion of the Martini as "just a drink for alcoholics" is only an extension of what Jimmy Carter had in mind when he denounced the opulent, expense-account Martini consumed by businessmen at the rate of three per lunch.

As the alcoholic's drink, the Martini has a function exactly the opposite of communal. It does not welcome the drinker into a brotherhood; it isolates him. This uncivilized Martini of the solitary alcoholic of course represents an extreme. It would be odd if the Martini were simply the combination of stark opposites, joyous harmony and solitary despair, and in fact the symbolism of this cocktail is far subtler and more complex. Between the Martinis of brotherhood and of solitary alcoholism lies a whole progression of Martinis that drinkers use against the world, but more or less harmlessly. In traversing this progression, as it approaches the state of being "just a drink for alcoholics," the Martini loses, little by little, its good character and becomes, not a civilized, but an uncivilized antidote to civilization.

When M. F. K. Fisher wrote that "a well-made Martini or Gibson, correctly chilled and nicely served, has been more often my true friend than any two-legged creature," she did not mean that she preferred to drink alone.[5] She spoke, rather, of the Martini that comforts the misfit, the solitary traveler, the loner, or the one who is world-weary or somehow at a loss. Any of these may take consolation in the Martini without reaching the far end of the progression, which belongs to the alcoholic.

A loner was Gordon Bassett (1890–1951), to whom Conrad Aiken addressed the elegy "Another Lycidas." The poem begins with the poet looking at a "photomatic photo" that Bassett had made while he was waiting for a train in Boston's South Station:

> Yet once more view
> the silent face whose fierce regard for you
> follows you like a conscience: stubborn, sober,
> who after two martinis waits
> and thus kills time till the opening of the gates.

The man, as he emerges in the rest of the poem, was a scholar who lived alone in a furnished room and led a disciplined life. Although Bassett's Martini was the loner's Martini, Aiken associates it, in the passage just quoted, with Bassett's moral qualities. The drink almost seems to confer stubbornness and sobriety on Bassett. Toward the end of the poem Aiken beautifully contrasts this Martini with the confraternal Martini of their earlier, roistering days, when they and their friends would visit the night spots of Boston and end up at the Athens-Olympia Restaurant on Stuart Street:

> to the Old Howard, or the Tam or Nip
> the Oyster House or Silver Dollar Bar
> then to the Athens, there once more to meet
> with Piston's whole-tone wit or Wheelwright's neat

while the martinis flow and clams are sweet
and he himself our morning star
until Apollo's taxi ploughs the dawn.[6]

The two Martinis that the sixty-one-year-old Bassett drank alone in South Station were of a different sort altogether.

In John Thomas's *Dry Martini: A Gentleman Turns to Love* the hero, Willoughby Quimby, uses the Martini not, like Bassett, as part of the regimen of scholarly asceticism but as a consolation for a meaningless lack of commitment. Quimby is leading the life of an Edwardian gentleman in the Paris of the 1920s. This is the Paris of the Right Bank, not the Left. The main action of the novel is framed by Martini-drinking scenes. When Quimby learns that his daughter, whom he has not seen since she was a child—she is now twenty—is coming to visit him, his confusion is such that he heads for "Dan's place," that is, the Ritz bar, and orders a dry Martini. He later takes a more optimistic view of his daughter's visit and hopes that it will be the beginning of a new, less dissolute life for him. He gives up his mistress, Georgette, and tries to stop drinking. The daughter, however, proves to be more sophisticated than the father had expected and goes off on her own, in quest of experience. Quimby, left alone with his daughter's traveling companion, falls in love with her and is rebuffed. Then he proposes marriage to a sweetheart of his youth and is rebuffed again. Finally, he tries to get his former wife, who is now in Paris on a holiday, to take him back, but she is planning to marry someone else. The novel ends thus:

> He stretched his arms as wide as the compass of the car permitted and felt, curiously, a new ease. One by one he had tried in vain every egress from the prison of his liberty, and now he was free again. The taxi paused before the swinging doors of Dan's place, and Mr. Quimby entered. The place was almost vacant at this hour and Mr. Quimby went straight to the bar. "Dry Martini, please, Dan," said Willoughby Quimby as he placed a contented foot upon the rail.[7]

The Martini stands for the whole way of life to which the thrice-jilted Quimby now happily returns. The positive isolating function of the Martini that appeared in the opening of Aiken's "Another Lycidas" can thus easily become negative. The Martini bestows on Quimby a passive, meaningless freedom.

But the negative isolating Martini can be active as well as passive— active and even aggressive. This is the Martini drunk by the greatest Martini-drinker in American fiction, Elam Harnish. He is the hero of Jack London's *Burning Daylight* of 1910. Burning Daylight is Elam Harnish's nickname, "which had been given him in his early days because of his habit of routing his comrades out of their blankets with the complaint that daylight was burning." Burning Daylight is born in Iowa, grows up in eastern Oregon, and in 1883, at age eighteen, crosses the Chilkoot Pass. He is thus one of the first prospectors in the Yukon. By age thirty he is an "elder hero" of the territory. He is a marvel of physical strength and endurance, of bravery, and of foresight. He foresees the locations of the big strikes, stakes a town site on the Stewart, and buys a third interest in another on the Klondike. When the strikes come, Burning Daylight makes $11 million on the development of these places. In about 1898 he sells out and goes down to San Francisco, where he begins a new career as entrepreneur. He first acquires some refinement: "He learned to eat and dress and generally comport himself after the manner of a civilized man."[8]

One of the first trappings of civilization that he acquires is the Martini. In New York, at a clandestine meeting of certain financiers, Burning Daylight orders a "cocktail": "Nobody seemed to notice the unusualness of a Martini at midnight, though Daylight looked sharply for that very thing; for he had long since learned that Martinis had their strictly appointed times and places. But he liked Martinis, and, being a natural man, he chose deliberately to drink when and how he pleased." When he learns that he has been swindled by these financiers, he goes to his hotel room and orders a Martini. After taking steps to recover his fortune, he returns to his hotel and has "one more cocktail for a nightcap." Jack London describes the change in his character after his return to San Francisco:

> In the swift rush of the game he found less and less time to spend on being merely good-natured. . . . His tremendous vitality remained, and radiated from all his being, but it was vitality under the new aspect of the man-trampling man-conqueror. His battles with elemental nature had been, in a way, impersonal; his present battles were wholly with the male of his species, and the hardships of the trail, the river, and the frost marred him far less than the bitter keenness of the struggle with his fellows. . . . In the North, he had drunk deeply and at irregular intervals; but now his drinking became systematic and disciplined. . . . Without reasoning or thinking about it, the strain of the office, which was essentially due to the daring and audacity of his ventures, required check or cessation; and he found, through the weeks and months, that cocktails supplied this very thing. They constituted a stone wall. He never drank during the morning, nor in office hours. . . . But the instant the business was finished, his everlasting call went out for a Martini, and for a double-Martini at that, served in a long glass so as not to excite comment.[9]

At this same time, Dede Mason, who is to be his salvation, enters his life, as his stenographer. Daylight is growing paunchy, drinks heavily, and immerses himself ever more deeply in business, so that he cannot even pursue his dawning interest in Dede. Upon the sudden death of one of his drinking companions, he reflects, "And when would his own turn come? Who could say? In the meantime, there was nothing to do but play the cards he could see in his hand, and they were *battle, revenge and cocktails.*" (The emphasis is Jack London's.) The cocktails, as we have already seen, are Martinis. But Daylight's growing attachment to Dede has a temperate effect. "The thought of her was like a cocktail. Or, at any rate, she substituted for a certain percentage of cocktails." This new form of intoxication does not last long. Daylight is deprived of his Sunday afternoon horseback rides with Dede, and at the same time he commences on the biggest deal of his life, the development of Oakland: "Every day brought its problems, and when he had solved them in his masterful way, he left the office in his big car, almost sighing with relief at the anticipation of the approaching double Martini." Dede continues to refuse to marry him, and his enterprise is threatened by a credit crunch:

> The strain he was under was terrific. . . . By the end of the day he was exhausted, and, as never before, he sought relief behind the wall of alcoholic inhibition [the stone wall of cocktails we have already heard about]. Straight to his hotel he was driven, and straight to his rooms he went, where immediately was mixed for him the first of a series of double Martinis.[10]

One morning he pauses to reflect on Dede's aphorism that you can only sleep in one bed at a time:

> The little woman's right. Only one bed at a time. . . . Thirty million dollars, and a hundred million or nothing in sight, and what have I got to show for it? There's lots of things that money can't buy. It can't buy the little woman. It can't buy capacity. What's the good of thirty million when I ain't got room for more than a quart of cocktails a day? . . . Here I am, a thirty times over millionaire, slaving harder every day than any dozen men that work for me, and all I get is two meals that don't taste good, one bed, a quart of Martini.

Daylight weathers the storm but at the last moment decides to let his position go, yield to his creditors, and retire to the farm in Sonoma that he still owns. He then goes to Dede and confesses that he had always loved cocktails, money, and himself more than her. But that is over. She is so impressed by his decision that she says she will marry him even if he does not sacrifice all his business interests. Daylight is astounded.

He asks, "You'll marry me if I keep working my head off and drinking Martinis?"[11] But he sticks to his plan. He and Dede withdraw to Sonoma and work the farm. Daylight forgets about drink, although he does not become a teetotaler. To oblige the local storekeeper, he sometimes takes one drink—of whiskey, which is what he had drunk on his occasional binges in the Yukon.

Thus, for Jack London in 1910, the Martini was already the drink of, even the weapon of, the embattled executive. In later days the connection of executive and Martini would become a theme for satire. In cartoons the executive works with a photograph of the Martini—not his wife or children—on his desk; he tells the bartender, "And make that Martini executive size" or "A Martini, Jack, very dry and to the point"; in an airplane he asks the stewardess, "And who, may I ask, determined that a dry Martini is a frill?" In a cartoon by Bernard Schoenbaum, a colossal statue of a Martini glass stands at the entrance to a corporate headquarters.[12]

The isolating function of the Martini has now appeared in the cases of the sober scholar Gordon Bassett; the dandy Willoughby Quimby; and the "man-trampling man-conqueror" Burning Daylight. These were all loners of one sort or another, by choice or by necessity. The Martini confirmed them in their aloneness, as consolation or support. For Daylight, it was a weapon. This isolating Martini is potentially, perhaps even essentially, uncivilized. The civilized antidote to civilization seems especially prone to misuse when it is taken in seclusion, apart from society, and that is because the Martini always carries with it the possibility of excess. John Doxat said, "There is no such thing as one Martini,"[13] and the answer to the old riddle is that a Martini is like a woman's breasts because one is not enough and three are too many. It was the conceit of *The Compleat Martini Cookbook* and *Son of the Martini Cookbook* that after the three or more Martinis that one would inevitably drink, only certain simple meals could be prepared, requiring only harmless utensils: "The recipes . . . are perfectly balanced to the alcoholic content of the human frame. Therefore we have no recipes geared to less than three martinis. . . . You will notice that the recipes become progressively simpler and we have tried to avoid the use of knives, graters or choppers as much as possible."[14]

As the excessive drink, the Martini is the characteristic choice of the alcoholic, as movies have always taught us. In *The Lost Weekend* (1945), the hero drinks Martinis while he plays "the solitary observant gentleman-drinker"—to quote from the novel on which the film was based—and steals the purse of the woman sitting next to him.[15] With the alcoholic, we reach the fulfillment of the uncivilized propensities of the Martini that were latent in the cases already studied.

Civilized and uncivilized

John F. Murray, in a 1977 story in the *New Yorker*, describes a scene in the Alcoholic Rehabilitation Unit of St. Julian's Hospital:

> Later on, in the dayroom, we move our chairs into a circle. A speaker from Alcoholics Anonymous has come to conduct a meeting for the patients. He is a nice-looking man who works for a television network. He tells us that he went to Miami as part of the crew covering a national convention but wound up drinking ice-cold Martinis every morning with some of the local station personnel. His boss back in New York heard about it and called him up and told him to come back and clean out his desk. Later, back in New York, he went to a girlfriend's apartment one night, drank with her, and ended up in the gutter in front of St. Clare's Hospital. He does not remember to this day how he got there.[16]

Here ends what the narrator calls the "drunkalogue." The man's fall was swift indeed after he drank those ice-cold Martinis in the morning. No other drink could have ruined him so quickly.

The alcoholic may appear to be, not the victim of a disease, but a willfully evil person, and the Martini can express the diabolic. An evil alcoholic was Canning, a character in Helen McCloy's 1951 mystery *Alias Basil Willing*. Canning is in cahoots with an even more evil German psychiatrist, Dr. Zimmer, who poisons his patients by arrangement with their relatives or the relatives by arrangement with the patients. The poison is administered in Martinis, which Dr. Zimmer serves in colored glasses at regular Friday evening dinner parties that he gives on the pretext of therapy. Canning is described driving into New York on his way to work:

> What he really needed now were two double Gibsons, very dry [a Gibson is a Martini with a small pickled onion instead of an olive or a piece of lemon peel]. Until he got those he didn't feel like a human being these days. He crossed the Triborough Bridge and slid in and out of traffic on the East River Drive. Too late to go to the office until afternoon now. Might as well have lunch at the Stardust Club. The drinks were good there. . . . He was taken to a small table marked "Reserved," though he hadn't made any reservation. A new waiter, young and inexperienced, handed him a luncheon menu. He waved it scornfully away and repeated his magic formula for health and happiness: "Two double Gibsons, very dry."

He then makes a telephone call to Dr. Zimmer and returns to his table:

> Back at his table, two frosted champagne glasses sat side by side, filled with an icy, oyster-white liquid that was almost pure gin with only a dash of vermouth. In each nestled a small, pallid onion. Canning drank thirstily, as if he were drinking water. Fire leapt through his arteries and warmed

his brain. His hand was steady when he reached for the second glass and his eyes were focusing perfectly.[17]

Whereas Gordon Bassett's two Martinis somehow increased his moral stature, Canning's two Gibsons and their grip on him are a sure sign of his depravity. If the loner is an alcoholic, the drink itself may become diabolical, as it is here, oyster-white with pallid onion, like a deadly mushroom. This is the proper drink for a man who is plotting the murder of his wife.[18]

White the Martini may be, but it is also noir. Indeed, in the pervasive return of noir style in the 1990s, the Martini shows its sinister side. Consider the collocation of Martini and cigarette in a Camel advertisement. Here is the description by William L. Hamilton in his article on noir style in the *New York Times:* "'What you're looking for,' reads the copy at the bottom of a Camel cigarette ad, which features a dark-lidded, 1990s femme fatale behind a martini glass in a shadowy lounge. The copy at the top of the picture is the Surgeon General's warning in letters as large as the sales pitch."[19] If you smoke, you may die. If you drink Martinis, you may die. This woman may kill you. This woman and the Martini may kill you. Smoke anyway. Drink anyway. Drink with her. In the illustration for the article from which I just quoted, two Martini glasses appear, one in the hands of a femme fatale, the other on a side table next to a small black purse with beaded strap. The caption calls the latter "Pottery Barn's name-your-poison martini glass." Dr. Zimmer would have taken that literally.

The alcoholic's Martini can easily be illustrated from real life. In an article in the *New York Times* of 1978, Ryne Duren, director of the Alcoholic Rehabilitation Department at Atroughton (Wisconsin) Community Hospital, describes his earlier life as an alcoholic. He was a relief pitcher for the New York Yankees in the late 1950s and early 1960s and then for other clubs. On what was to be his last day in baseball, when he was working for the old Washington Senators, he was called in to pitch against the Yankees. Laboring under a massive hangover, he gave up two runs on a wild pitch that hit the ground ten feet in front of home plate and bounced over the catcher's head; he hit two batters and walked another; then he gave up a double to Mickey Mantle. Afterward, in the clubhouse, he drank six or eight beers. Duren says, "Then, after the game, I went to the Winsor Park Hotel and had a few vodka martinis. I started feeling good, and then I started feeling sorry for myself. I wallowed in self-pity. My marriage had broken up, my fastball wasn't effective anymore, my knee was giving me trouble. And I was a lush."[20] A baseball player drinking Martinis? That in itself shows that something is wrong.[21]

Baseball and the Martini have nothing to do with each other, as the experience of Roger Angell, a baseball writer for the *New Yorker,* showed. He decided to watch the 1963 World Series on television, each game in a different bar. He watched the first game in O'Leary's Bar at Fifty-third Street and Eighth Avenue. The place was packed with beer-drinking Yankees fans in shirt-sleeves. They were such connoisseurs of baseball that they were more pleased at having seen Koufax break the strike-out record than they were depressed at the Yankees' loss. The second game found Angell in Charles Cafe on Forty-third Street, just west of Vanderbilt Avenue. Here the patrons wore suits and ties and showed slight interest in the spectacle unfolding on the television screen. To illustrate the difference between the two bars and their clientele, Angell wrote, "One junior executive next to me at the bar ordered a . . . dry Martini on the rocks—a drink that has perhaps never been served in O'Leary's."[22] The Martini here epitomizes indifference to baseball.

The Martini and baseball are irreconcilable, and for this reason Ryne Duren could use the drink as a way of signifying to himself and perhaps also to others that his career as a baseball player was over. But not only did the Martini say, "I am no longer a baseball player," it also said, "I *am* an alcoholic." The Martini had been defined as the alcoholic's drink in movies, literature, and popular belief long before Ryne Duren sat down at the bar in the Winsor Park Hotel.

Plate 1.
The Lalique Martini glass,
1997. Photograph courtesy of
Lalique.

Plate 2.
Michael Jaross Martini glasses,
1997. Photograph by Roger
Schreiber.

Plate 3.
Hilton McConnico's Martini
glass for Bombay Sapphire Gin,
1997. Advertisement ©
Carillon Importers. Reprinted
by permission.

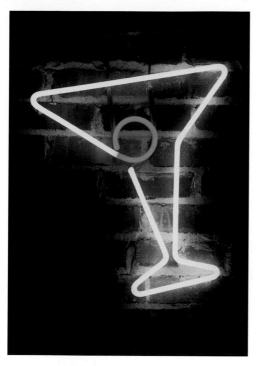

Plate 4.
Neon Martini glass on brick
wall by Bill Concannon,
Aargon Neon, Crockett, Calif.,
1997. Photograph by Glen
Millward.

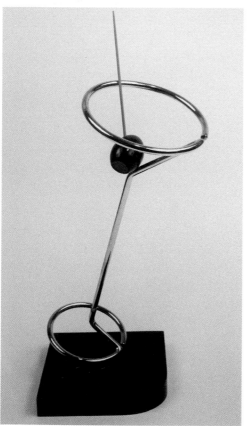

Plate 5.
Claes Oldenburg, *Tilting
Neon Cocktail,* 1983. Stainless
steel, cast aluminum,
acrylic paint, and Plexiglas.
19 x 10 x 10 inches.
Photograph courtesy of
PaceWildenstein.

Plate 6.
De Beers advertisement from
the 1980s. Photograph by
Jack Abraham. Reprinted by
permission.

The Martini unites—
the Martini separates

IN THE ALCOHOLIC, the isolating function of the Martini reaches an extreme and the drink's uncivilized potential is fulfilled. Against this diabolic drink, which can even be the vehicle of poison, must be set its counterpart, the civilized Martini, which is the drink of love and friendship.

As the drink of love, the Martini marks all the stages of the relationship between man and woman from inception to breakup or marriage. Brian Kelly, the hero of John Leonard's *The Naked Martini* (1964), who is second only to Burning Daylight among the Martini-drinkers of American fiction, ordered Martinis on his first date with Jill and offered a forward-looking toast, "To our relationship."[1] So too four decades earlier, in John Dos Passos's *Manhattan Transfer,* the Martini marks the beginning. Ellen, also called Elaine, who has been the central figure in this episodic and many-charactered novel, meets George Baldwin at a hotel. George has loved her through all her marriages and affairs, and through his own unsuccessful marriage. This is the climax of their stories. She arrives forty-five minutes late and says to him, "You go in and order anything you like. I'm going to the ladies' room a minute. . . . And please have me a Martini. I'm dead tonight, just dead." George obediently goes into the dining room and says, "Well Joseph what are you going to give us to eat tonight? I'm hungry. . . . But first you can get Fred to make the best Martini cocktail he ever made in his life." When Ellen comes to the table, George begins to discuss the marriage to which Ellen has already consented:

She leaned over and patted his hand that grasped the edge of the table. "George let's eat our dinner first. . . . We've got to be sensible. God knows we've messed things up enough in the past both of us. . . . Let's drink to the crime wave." The smooth infinitesimal foam of the cocktail was soothing in her tongue and throat, glowed gradually warmly through her. She looked at him with sparkling eyes. He drank his at a gulp. "By gad Elaine," he flamed up helplessly, "you're the most wonderful thing in the world."[2]

The glow inspired by the Martini-of-the-relationship was also felt by Colonel Cantwell, the hero of Hemingway's *Across the River and into the Trees* (1950). The grizzled colonel meets his nineteen-year-old girlfriend in Harry's Bar in Venice:

"Waiter," the Colonel called; then asked, "Do you want a dry Martini, too?"
"Yes," she said. "I'd love one."
"Two very dry Martinis," the Colonel said. "Montgomerys. Fifteen to one."
The waiter, who had been in the desert, smiled and was gone, and the Colonel turned to Renata.
"You're nice," he said: "You're also very beautiful and lovely and I love you."

After further billing and cooing, the narrative resumes: "The Martinis were icy cold and true Montgomerys, and, after touching the edges, they felt them glow happily all through their upper bodies."[3] The Montgomery, by the way, is so named because, according to the colonel, General Montgomery would not attack unless his troops outnumbered the enemy's fifteen to one. Thus the waiter's knowing smile.

Another Martini-of-the-relationship appears in Evelyn Waugh's *Brideshead Revisited* (1945). The narrator of the novel, Charles Ryder, begins an affair with Julia on a transatlantic crossing. She is the sister of Sebastian, his Oxford friend, and he had met her at her family's estate, Brideshead, years before. It is now the late 1930s. On a train from London, returning to Brideshead, they go to the dining car:

The knives and forks jingled on the tables as we sped through the darkness; the little circle of gin and vermouth in the glasses lengthened to oval, contracted again, with the sway of the carriage, touched the lip, lapped back again, never spilt; I was leaving the day behind me. Julia pulled off her hat and tossed it into the rack above her, and shook her night-dark hair with a little sigh of ease—a sigh fit for the pillow, the sinking firelight and a bedroom window open to the stars and the whisper of bare trees.[4]

The Martini, Julia's action, and the reveries she inspires in Charles are not causally connected here, but the Martini often means, if a couple is drinking it, that it's time for bed.

In short, the Martini is an aphrodisiac, and of course a man can use it as such, as does Anthony Patch, the hero of F. Scott Fitzgerald's *The Beautiful and the Damned* (1922). He amuses himself with Geraldine Burke, an usher in a theater, while he waits to marry Gloria, who is of his own station, and he plies the poor girl with Martinis: "It was Monday and Anthony took Geraldine Burke to luncheon at the Beaux Arts— afterward they went up to his apartment and he wheeled out the little rolling table that held his supply of liquor, selecting vermuth *[sic]*, gin, and absinthe for a proper stimulant."[5] The spelling out of the ingredients, as in a witch's chant, reflects the fact that it is a potion.

The couples in the Seagram's advertisements of the 1970s, well dressed, self-assured, primly holding their stemmed Martini glasses, do not look as if they will soon be playing the two-backed beast, and yet because of the Martinis, the suggestion is inescapable.[6] In fact, the Martinis are all that is needed, in an otherwise unsuggestive setting, to make that suggestion. The Martini is already defined in popular belief as a love potion. M. F. K. Fisher, in one of her gastronomic works, prescribes a Martini for herself at the beginning of a meal that "would culminate in the flowering of mutual desire."[7] In the film *The Graduate* (1967), when Mrs. Robinson (Anne Bancroft) goes to the Taft Hotel to begin her affair with Benjamin (Dustin Hoffman), she orders a Martini. A poem attributed to Dorothy Parker expresses the idea directly:

I like to have a Martini,
Two at the very most.
After three I'm under the table,
After four I'm under my host![8]

In a 1979 diatribe against having children, Cleveland Amory remarks despairingly of one of his friends, "You give Tubby that third martini and the next thing you know he's having another baby."[9]

That the Martini is an aphrodisiac is obvious enough. The Martini also plays a part in other phases of the relationship. In Renata Adler's 1976 *Speedboat*, an old, too solid affair is almost mirrored in the drink:

We had ordered martinis, straight up, with a twist of lemon. The waitress had brought martinis with olives. This had the force of an *éclaircissement.* "Not exactly a twist of lemon," I said when she had left. "No," Jim said, "it isn't." That was it. I have known Jim, after all, a long time. I still make these inane attempts to have a conversation.[10]

Unites and separates

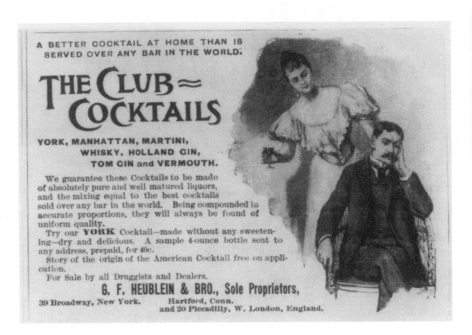

« FIGURE 3 »
Wife administers cocktail to fatigued husband
From Puck, 12 Dec. 1894, 300

It is not clear where these Martinis will lead, but in Dorothy Parker's 1942 story "Dusk before Fireworks," the end is near. The high-strung sophisticate Kit visits the apartment of the handsome philanderer Hobie. He receives a telephone call from another woman, and she retires into the bathroom:

> When she returned, eventually, to the living-room, the young man was pouring pale, cold liquid into small glasses. He gave one to her, and smiled at her over it. It was his wistful smile. It was one of his best.

By a nice reticence, Dorothy Parker never names the drink, but it is one of the most fixed conventions of American literature that the Martini-of-the-relationship must be commented upon by the characters or by the author, and she does not break this convention. After Kit says a few words about how indifferent she is to the telephone call, Hobie replies with "Oh."

> "Oh," he said, and tried his cocktail. "Is this dry enough, sweet? Because you like them dry, don't you? Sure it's all right? Ah, wait a second, darling. Let *me* light your cigarette. There. Sure you're all right?"[11]

« FIGURE 4 »
Three-quarters of a century after 1894 (Figure 3), things
are worse for the husband, but the Martini is still there to console him
Lee Lorenz © 1969 from The New Yorker Collection.
All rights reserved.

This relationship is coming to an unhappy end, but the Martini can also
be present when a relationship ends with a proposal of marriage. In
Sara Davidson's *Loose Change* (1978), Sara describes meeting Michael at
Sardi's:

> I wore a red wool mini, black tights and black boots and felt sensational
> as the captain showed me to the table. "Why don't you have a martini?"
> Michael said. "Okay." I was looking around happily and the two actors at
> the next table were staring. When the drinks came I immediately took a
> sip. "What's that in the glass?" he asked.
> "Hmmmm?"
> "In the glass."
> "Nothing."
> "For God's sake, look again."
> I peered into it. At the bottom was a diamond ring.[12]

The ultimate Martini-of-the-relationship carries a diamond engagement
ring, just as the isolating Martini, in its harshest form, carried Dr. Zimmer's dose of poison.

The Martini is also the drink of the married couple, although now its
function is not aphrodisiacal but restorative. In the evening the wife
awaits her husband at the door with a Martini. This was the picture of
marriage in the mind of John Leonard's Brian Kelly, and Bernard DeVoto,

Unites and separates

in his famous celebration of the Martini, said that the cocktail hour "needs a wife of similar impulse."[13] The wife at the door inevitably became the theme of cartoons that explored all the comical possibilities of the conjugal Martini,[14] and these cartoons complement the other main type, the hard-charging Martini-drinking executive. Or perhaps it is really only one type, with the same Martini-drinker in different situations. De Beers combined the two ideas in the advertisement for its "Diamond Anniversary Ring": a photograph of a band of diamonds on the olive in a Martini on the rocks, with the message, "For all the times the ice melted waiting for me to come home" (Plate 6).[15] The wife had dutifully prepared her husband's Martini, but he, the busy executive, was detained at the office.

The Martini-of-the-relationship looks, then, both to eros and to conjugal harmony, as well as to intermediate stages. The two extremes, eros and marriage, are combined in bizarre fashion in the following dirty joke:

> Two men driving down a street one day noticed a pair of dogs copulating. One man said to the other, "Gee, I wish I could prevail upon my wife to do it that way." The other said, "That's easy. Just give her three Martinis and she'll do it any way you want." The man said, "Well, maybe I should try that." About a week later, they met again and the man who had given the advice asked, "Well, did you try the Martinis? How did you get along?" The man replied, "Well, I got along very well, but you were way off on your count—I had to give her five Martinis just to get her out on the front lawn."

The humor is complex. On the one hand, the punch line depends upon the unexpectedness of the front lawn as the aspect of canine copulation that especially attracted the man. On the other hand, the Martini as an aphrodisiac *within*—that is, not *before*—marriage is a grotesquely unconventional application, humorous in itself, of this cocktail. After marriage, the Martini is no longer used for seduction but is rather an almost maternal consolation offered by wife to husband. The image has not faded. It continues not only in advertisements, like the one for the "Diamond Anniversary Ring," but also, right up to the 1990s, in *New Yorker* cartoons.[16]

The conjugal Martini is just one form of the communal middle-class Martini that is mixed and drunk at home with wife and friends. The great distinction of this Martini is that it is the centerpiece of a rite, the elaborateness of which is rivaled only by the rite of the Mint Julep.[17] In its rite, the Martini exercises a communal function. The host or paterfamilias who mixes the drinks acts as priest, and families or friends are united as devotees of the cult. DeVoto's "For the Wayward and Beguiled," which provides the *locus classicus* for the middle-class Martini, is permeated with a sense of ritual, and his strictures have a distinctly priestly air about them.[18] By contrast, the loner's Martini seems even lonelier, and the loner may even, in an extreme case, be led to a perversion of the rite. The director Fritz Lang (1890–1976), not merely a loner but by all accounts a misanthrope, served Martinis to an articulated wooden ape to which he was so devoted that it was buried with him.[19]

The rite has its paraphernalia: the ice bucket, the distinctive glass, the shaker or pitcher, the glass rod, the olives, and the lemon and *zesteur* or knife, if a twist of lemon is to be the garnish. Only the priest knows how to mix the cocktail. He will use the same utensils each time. The ceremony is spoiled if something is missing and a substitute is required. Each cult, in a bar or in a household, will have its own hors d'oeuvres, served in small sizes and consumed sparingly. Nourishment is not their purpose.[20] Like the utensils, they are always the same. Once upon a time, the smoking of cigarettes would have been de rigueur. It all seems very civilized, but in the withering perspective of the psycho-historico-anthropologist, it is a symbolic blood covenant or perhaps goes back to the sealing of vows with alcoholic beverages.[21] The Owl Club ritual (Simple Message 6) is probably a pale survival.

The ritual appears in a comic form in *The Discreet Charm of the Bourgeoisie* (1972), directed by Luis Buñuel (1900–1983). François Thévenot, a businessman, mixes Martinis at the home of the Sénéchals while he, his wife, and two friends wait for their hosts to appear. (The Sénéchals are climbing down the trellis from their bedroom, in order to make love somewhere outside. This maneuver is necessary because Mrs. Sénéchal screams when she makes love.) Like many a Martini ritualist, Thévenot gives a pedantic commentary as he makes the drink. He complains that the glasses on the tray before him are not the right ones: "Idéal pour le dry Martini c'est le verre classique en forme de cône" (The ideal thing for a dry Martini is the classic glass in the shape of a cone). Just as he finishes his sentence, one of his friends appears with the classic glasses. (She has obviously heard the speech on other occasions.) He continues: "D'abord dans l'importance c'est la glace. Il faut qu'elle soit d'excéllente qualité, très froide, très dure—exactement comme celle-ci" (The ice is of prime importance. It must be of excellent quality, very cold, very hard—exactly like this here). The others do not seem to be interested in what he is saying.[22] (The contrast between the overrefined Thévenot and the passionate Sénéchals is hard to miss.)

The proper vessel is an indispensable element in the ritual—"le verre classique en forme de cône." Difficult historical questions surround the glass. At what point did it come into use? At what point did it become identified with the Martini, and with the Martini's brother, the Manhattan? The form appears in the 1920s and is associated with the Martini in advertising in the 1930s. The Thin Man movies, which began in 1934, do not provide the evidence that one might have expected; there, the Martini is served in several different glasses. I have answered the questions, as best I can, in the appendix. As for the history of the rite as a whole, it is relatively clear and is dealt with in "Historical Background of the Ambiguities."

The Martini is classic—
the Martini is individual

"P ERFECT" is an adjective that the Martini readily attracts, as in the title
The Perfect Martini Book.[1] With its minimal ingredients and simple
preparation, it ought to be capable of perfection. There ought to be the
one perfect Martini, which should always be mixed. The engagingly dif-
fident bartender in a cartoon tells his customer, "The perfect Martini.
Failing that, the near-perfect Martini."[2] But within the very simplicity of
the Martini there is room for apparently infinite variation. The Martini
is thus proverbial for idiosyncrasy. An article in the 1978 Home section
of the *Boston Globe* begins, "Taking care of floors . . . is a little like making Martinis: Everyone you meet has a different formula."[3]

Compounders of Martinis therefore direct their efforts in two opposite directions. Either they try to make the classic or perfect Martini
that would, hypothetically, be the choice of all Martini drinkers; or they
seek some individual nuance that makes their own Martini unique. This
thing, whatever it may be, is their "secret," which they would not wish
to become universal.

Advertising has encouraged both tendencies. In the late 1960s, Gordon's promoted "The Personaltini." "At last!" the copy ran, "A Martini
dry enough to bear your name!" Each advertisement carried forty-five
first names, each with the suffix *-tini*: Albertini, Alicetini, Babetini, and
so forth. At the same time, the recommended Martini was Gordon's Gin
poured "lovingly" on the rocks, vermouth to taste, and forget about the
garnishes. In other words, a completely impersonal Martini. What the
drink itself lacked in individuality was supplied by the conceit, or impos-
ture, that one's choice of Gordon's created ipso facto a "Personaltini."

During the same period, Seagram's took another approach to the individual Martini. Their advertisements purported to reveal the closely guarded secrets of Martini-drinkers. One of the full-page layouts carried the photograph of an urbane, intelligent-looking couple. The caption read, "Our secret? A pinch of salt on top of each martini." (A Martini-of-the-relationship is, of course, implied in all this, too.)[4]

The secrets are almost endless. They can be roughly divided into liquids and solids. The liquids that have been added to Martinis, besides the bitters and absinthe that were once standard, are grenadine, sherry, cider, *sake,* coffee liqueur, Chanel No. 5, rose water, sauterne, Liebfraumilch, and Scotch. The solids, in addition to various sorts of olives, lemon peel, and pearl onions, are mint, garlic, shrimps, anchovies, various nuts, small pickled artichoke hearts, red caviar, grapes, tiny eggplants, tiny green tomatoes, button mushrooms, and crystallized violets. These lists are only long enough to suggest further novelties that more strenuous research would surely uncover. Another garnish became the object of a cult in Washington, D.C., in 1959 and was reported in *Time.* The garnish was a two-inch green bean, pickled in dill vinegar, which produced the "dillytini."[5]

For the most part the very nature of the Martini thwarts such monograms. A cartoon in the *New Yorker* shows a stout, bald, self-important man who sits down at a bar, puts his hands on the edge of the bar, and says to the bartender, "I'd like a very dry Martini straight up, and bring a little something of yourself to it, Louie."[6] The request is ludicrous because the Martini, especially the dry Martini straight up, is a classic. As such, it resists the pompous intrusion of personality, and all attempts to find some clever, individual garnish are doomed in advance.

The water of which the ice is made may be chosen in the name of the classic or perfect Martini, or it may be another "secret." In either case the reality that underlies the Martini-mixer's choice of distilled water, bottled spring water, or Perrier or the like for his ice is that what comes out of the tap in most American cities is undrinkable. Since the Martini "straight up" contains some—and the Martini on the rocks a lot of—meltage, some alternative supply must be found. Mr. George A. Macomber, a former president of the Cambridge Trust Company, tells an anecdote about the Martini-drinker's ice in an essay on his bank that he contributed to the *Proceedings* of the Cambridge Historical Society. He writes about dining with a director of the bank in the early 1930s:

> I recall my first dinner party at the Berkeley Place house of David H. Howe. . . . He was, and still is, a wise and notable gourmet whose knowledge of wines made him lift his eyebrows at too many cocktails. He used, however, to serve one Martini before his dinners. When I praised the one

« FIGURE 5 »
Membership certificate,
Lower Montgomery Street Olive or Onion Society, mid-1950s
Photograph by Jack Malnati

he handed me, he remarked, "If its flavor is different from those you make, it's because I feel you can't use ice made from Cambridge water, on account of the chlorine content. My Martini ice is made from Belmont Springs Company's water.[7]

Mr. Howe's strictures on water nicely illustrate the ambivalence of this ingredient in the Martini. On the one hand, Belmont Springs water is his "secret"; on the other, he implies that this water is necessary for the perfect Martini that all men should strive to attain.

The perfect Martini is, of course, the standard that gin manufacturers have usually held up to drinkers of this cocktail. Their advertisements say, in effect, that the perfect Martini can be attained only by the use of their gin. For example, "the unhesitating verdict of men of the greatest experience is that Booth's House of Lords is the *essential* ingredient of the perfect Martini."[8] Although it may be *chacun à son goût* in every other area of food and drink, the Martini is measured on a severe, objective scale. We may drink Martinis, think that we are enjoying them, and be oblivious to the fact that the perfect Martini is something that we have not come close to mixing. In the meantime, "men of the

Classic and individual
61

greatest experience" or other superior beings may have found the perfect Martini without our knowing it.

Such thoughts could have inspired the Martini contest held by a liquor distributor in Chicago in 1951. The contest, which was reported in *Life* but not, for some reason, in the *Chicago Tribune*, drew 240 contestants, each with a different recipe. The aim of the contest was to discover the "best" Martini recipe, which was to be published, along with twenty-four runners-up, by the promoter. *Life* printed the winning recipe, which called for an olive stuffed with an anchovy and a glass rinsed with Cointreau.[9] One feels that the quest for perfection somehow ended in a nugatory stab at individuality.

A more rational quest for perfection was undertaken at about the same time by a group in San Francisco who called themselves the Lower Montgomery Street Olive or Onion Society. The impulse came from Mr. Barney Vogel, who held Martini-tastings in his home. The results were submitted to a panel of three hotel men at Ricky's Town House on Van Ness Avenue, September 29, 1953. The panel chose a surprisingly bland Martini made with three parts gin and one part Cresta Blanca White Vermouth. Hereupon the Cresta Blanca Wine Company joined the fun and used the L.M.S.O. or O. Society in its advertising for the next five years. Neither the society nor any of its members received any compensation, since they wished to remain true to their original purpose, which was amusement, their own and others'. Messrs. Vogel, Willard Cox, Tom Collard, and Paul Nyeland, the grand exalted master tasters, created a nonresident membership, with a handsome certificate and membership card. There were no dues, no committees, no election, and only the shadowiest governance. Mr. Nyeland described the broader society of nonresident members thus:

> Membership in the organization is somewhat like being part of the Kentucky Colonels group, which also has no formal organization or meeting hall. It's a spiritual thing. You know that any time you are sipping a martini, somewhere another member is probably doing the same thing and thinking of you. It's a good feeling.[10]

Here is as strong a statement of the communal force of the Martini as one can find. The desire to find the perfect or classic Martini arises, then, in those for whom the Martini is the communal drink, the sacramental drink that unites in spirit even those who have never met. Contrariwise, those who seek the individual nuance, those who have a "secret," are obviously drinkers of the isolating Martini. They are heretics who do not participate in the rite. The third ambiguity therefore converges with the first. The Martini is civilized and classic; the Martini is uncivilized and individual.

The Martini is sensitive—
the Martini is tough

THE MARTINI is in itself both sensitive and tough. DeVoto's essay contains a characteristic appreciation of the sensitivity of this cocktail:

> You can no more keep a martini in the refrigerator than you can keep a kiss there. The proper union of gin and vermouth is a great and sudden glory; it is one of the happiest marriages on earth, and one of the shortest-lived. The fragile tie of ecstasy is broken in a few minutes, and thereafter there can be no remarriage.[1]

The sensitivity of the Martini is more commonly encountered in the form of the belief that it makes a difference if the gin is poured into the pitcher before the vermouth or vice versa, or that the Martini cannot be shaken because the gin or the vermouth or both will be bruised. Robin Maugham reports these words of his uncle: "'Martinis should never be shaken,' he said. 'They should always be stirred so that the molecules lie sensuously on top of each other.'"[2]

The difference between shaking and stirring is, in reality, negligible, and the choice of one method or the other rests on the superstition that the nature of the drink is somehow affected. Unlike other ceremonial aspects of the Martini-rite, this superstition is directly related to the sensitivity of the drink itself, to its supposed capacity for being injured by malpractice. Historically, both methods have had their vogues. More than a hundred years ago Leo Engel wrote, "Tastes differ. An Indian likes a cocktail swizzled; a North American, within the last few years, will not take one unless it is stirred with a spoon; a South American will have it shaken; an Englishman, who has traveled in America, is more particular than any of the others until you find out his taste, and is most difficult to please."[3]

In 1934, however, A. S. Crockett spoke of shaking as if it had superseded stirring: "Modern practice prescribes shaking for a Dry Martini. This, however, weakens the mixture and used to be discountenanced by barmen who believed in tradition."[4] What Crockett said of modern practice is borne out by a letter of the late Clarence Brigham, who was director of the American Antiquarian Society and an amateur historian of the cocktail. He wrote on November 23, 1948, to Mr. George A. Zabriskie, "An old-time drinker told me that cocktails had always been stirred, whereas I distinctly remember that forty years ago both Manhattans and Martinis were shaken."[5] And yet the three Martini recipes that I have seen from the first decade of the twentieth century all require stirring, as do most of the scores of later recipes. Probably stirring was always normal—it was, as Leo Engel said, the North American taste—while shaking had its moments. In any case, the choice of one method or the other has always depended upon a belief in the Martini's capacity for alteration or injury, a belief that has no foundation in reality and is thus characteristic of this symbolic and myth-laden cocktail.

While the Martini-mixer believes that he can affect the drink, he also believes that the drink can affect him, and more powerfully than he can affect it. The Martini is tougher than it is sensitive. The toughness of the Martini lies in its punch. The Martini-drinker and others believe that the Martini is a drink of unique power. Berton Roueche spoke of "the almost mystical awe in which the Martini is commonly held" and explained that a Martini "is no more, and no less, intoxicating than any other drink that contains the same amount of alcohol."[6] This statement is substantiated by experiments conducted by Dr. Giorgio Lolli and associates in 1941 and in 1964. The earlier experiment showed that Martinis and whiskey produce about the same blood alcohol curve. The electroencephalographic and electromyographic tracings gathered in 1964 hinted that wine, in comparison with Martinis, caused a decreased receptivity to external stimuli.[7] In one sense, then, wine was found to be stronger than Martinis. On the other hand, Dr. Lolli wrote to me, the Martini "seemed to contribute to neutralize the inconveniences of a long experimental session."

But no amount of experimental data will change the Martini's reputation for power. The Martini is nicknamed "the silver bullet" because of its supposedly lethal properties. In particular, silver is prescribed for killing supernatural demons like witches, vampires, and werewolves, as Adrienne Mayor pointed out to me, and thus corresponds to the purifying, apotropaic function of the Martini. The nickname also seems to contain a hint of the Martini's sensitivity. Although this cocktail is a lethal bullet, it is made of silver, not of some base metal.

The two sides of the Martini, sensitive and tough, were well expressed in an advertisement for Bengal Gin that appeared in the *New Yorker* in 1967.[8] Next to the bottle of gin, the label of which bore the head of a fierce Bengali tiger, stood a Martini glass, and on the surface of the drink shimmered the reflection of the tiger. The laws of optics were somewhat strained to make the point that the tiger's characteristics were embodied in the Martini made with Bengal Gin. Beneath the bottle and the glass there was a caption: "Beauty and the Beast." Here, in so many words, is the ambiguity of the Martini.

The Martini-drinker has, of course, the same characteristics as the drink itself. A few years before the advertisement for Bengal Gin appeared, W. H. Auden wrote:

Could any tiger
Drink martinis, smoke cigars,
And last as we do?[9]

We who drink Martinis and smoke cigars are tougher than a tiger. This proposition is put, however, in the delicate form of a haiku, a seventeen-syllable stanza borrowed from Japanese poetry. We are also sensitive. The haiku is a poetic form ideally suited to the Martini, having a strict formula and yet admitting individuality.

The cigar, be it noted, has often served to overdetermine the Martini's toughness. Jake Offutt, the politician in Sinclair Lewis's *Babbitt,* has already been heard (Ambiguity 1). The comedian George Burns (1896–1996) attributed his longevity to cigars and Martinis.[10] His attitude is expressed in a cartoon by Lorenz in the *New Yorker* in 1997. A couple walks past a restaurant called "STEAKS, MARTINIS & CIGARS." A sign under the restaurant's name says, "YOU GOT A PROBLEM WITH THAT?"[11] Curiously, the pairing of Martini and cigar can also express sensitivity, that of the gentleman connoisseur. In 1986, *Esquire* carried on the same page instructions on how to make a Martini and how to smoke a cigar.[12] After his book on the Martini, Barnaby Conrad published one on the cigar.[13]

James Bond drank Martinis, usually of vodka, in most of the novels by Ian Fleming that appeared at the rate of one a year from 1953 to 1961, and he is remembered for the injunction "shaken, not stirred." By this he displayed his toughness and deliberate insensitivity to the concern for the molecules that W. S. Maugham felt. Bond was also possessed, however, of considerable sensitivity in the areas of food, drink, and women. In some of the novels he was on the verge of falling in love, and in *Casino Royale* he considered marrying the girl and giving up his profession. It was also in this novel that he invented a special Martini, to which he gave the girl's name:

> "A dry martini," he said. "One. In a deep champagne goblet."
>
> "Oui, monsieur."
>
> "Just a moment. Three measures of Gordon's, one of vodka, half a measure of Kina Lillet.[14] Shake it very well until it's ice-cold, then add a large thin slice of lemon-peel. Got it?"
>
> "Certainly, monsieur." The barman seemed pleased with the idea.
>
> "Gosh, that's certainly a drink," said Leiter [Bond's CIA counterpart].
>
> Bond laughed. "When I'm . . . er . . . concentrating," he explained, "I never have more than one drink before dinner. But I do like that one to be large and very strong and very cold and very well-made. . . . This drink's my own invention. I'm going to patent it when I can think of a good name."

Later he meets the girl of the novel and learns her name: Vesper Lynd.

> "I think it's a fine name," said Bond. An idea struck him. "Can I borrow it?" He explained about the special martini he had invented, and his search for a name for it. "The Vesper," he said. "It sounds perfect and it's very appropriate to the violet hour when my cocktail will now be drunk all over the world. Can I have it?"[15]

At the end, Vesper Lynd commits suicide. It is the only way out, since she, a double agent, has now fallen in love with James Bond. Was it because of the beautiful double agent's memory that James Bond never drank "the Vesper" again? The drink itself, however, did not die. The invention of the redoubtable 007 was mixed by the American aristocrat, Paul Mellon. "Offered a drink, the guests follow the suggestion of a special martini combining gin and vodka with an innuendo of vermouth."[16]

James Bond is exceeded in both sensitivity and toughness by Colonel Cantwell, who drank the Martini-of-the-relationship with his nineteen-year-old girlfriend, Renata. Hemingway's colonel is, on the one hand, an aesthete. He has opinions on art, architecture, and literature. He likes his room to be tidy, and he has an acute sense of punctilio. On the other hand, he is awesomely tough, and he admires toughness above all else, except, perhaps, for female beauty. En route to Venice, where the action of the novel is set, he tells his driver about the city: "The people are very tough."[17] He and the driver then debate the question, Which is the toughest town in the United States? The colonel has killed 122 men. These were sure kills; there may have been more. He is covered with scars from his participation in two world wars. In Venice he beats up sailors who whistle at his girlfriend. When he looks in the mirror, he sees "a basically kind mouth which could be truly ruthless." Physical courage is natural to him, since he believes that "death is a lot of shit." He often reflects on his "wild-boar truculence." He asks himself, "Why am I always a bastard?" And he prays, "God help me to avoid brutality."

The *miles gloriosus,* or braggart soldier, a stock literary figure since antiquity, is typically as bibulous as he is boastful, and the colonel is no exception. Upon reaching the parking garage outside Venice, he has Gordon's and Campari at the bar. At his hotel, before going up to his room, he downs two double Martinis. He orders the drink, "*secco, molto secco e doppio.*" In his room, he has more gin and Campari. Then he meets Renata at Harry's and has three Montgomerys. With dinner, they—but one gathers that he does most of the drinking—have a bottle of Capri Bianco and one of Valpolicella, followed by two of champagne (Roederer '42). They take another bottle of champagne (Perrier-Jouet) with them in the gondola. Floating along the canals, they make love twice, and the lusty old colonel is ready for a third attempt, but Renata dissuades him; it may be bad for his ailing heart. Back in his hotel room, the colonel finds Valpolicella set out for him. He drinks two bottles in the course of the night. When he goes to the bathroom in the morning he takes a glass of wine with him. The waiter who comes to the colonel's room with the breakfast menu brings a decanter of Valpolicella, from "the big wicker fiascos of two liters" preferred by the colonel because they remind him of the old days. When Renata joins him later, she has her breakfast, and he has another decanter of Valpolicella. Later that morning, they go to Harry's for Martinis before lunch. Back at the Gritti, they have more Valpolicella and a *vino secco* from Vesuvius. When the colonel leaves that afternoon to participate in a duck-shoot, he takes a flask of Gordon's and washes down his pills with gin. After the shoot, he drinks grappa.

In all this, the Martinis are clearly the *pièce de résistance.* The colonel drinks a total of five of them on the day of his arrival in Venice and two the next day. The rest is wine and an occasional slug of gin, with or without Campari. His Martini is partly, of course, the Martini-of-the-relationship, but that is not all. His Martini is tough and sensitive too, drunk as it is by such a tough man in a town the toughness of which excites his admiration and the beauty of which often touches his sensibilities.

Let us now consider the Martini in Hemingway's *Islands in the Stream.*[18] The bibulous old braggadocio, Thomas Hudson. . . . No. Instead, please read Daniel Hardy's send-up of Hemingway, "The Last Good Martini," reprinted at the end of this section.

The fourth ambiguity is different from the first three in that both the opposite traits, toughness and sensitivity, may coexist in the drink at the same time for the same person, as for a man of Colonel Cantwell's complexity. The two sides of the ambiguity are usually reflected, however, in the difference between two sorts of Martini-drinker. W. S. Maugham drank the sensitive, James Bond the tough, Martini.

John Doxat's *Stirred—Not Shaken: The Dry Martini* contains a valuable reminiscence of Maugham. Mauro Lotti, now the barman at the Grand Hotel in Rome, once held the same position at the Beau Rivage in Lausanne, whither Maugham would repair after his visits to Professor Niemans's clinic. Signor Lotti recalls that Maugham "used to drink a Dry Martini as if it were a rite, and he tasted it in the same way he enjoyed his cigarettes, without filter, and smoked to the last bit held with fingers tired and yellowed, that looked almost golden."[19] Maugham was drinking the civilized Martini, the one that is the centerpiece of a rite. With his concern for the molecules, for proper mixing, he also showed himself a devotee of the classic Martini. The example of Maugham shows, therefore, how one side of the fourth ambiguity, sensitivity, converges with one side of each of the first and the third ambiguities: the Martini is sensitive and civilized and classic.

James Bond, on the other hand, was a drinker of the tough Martini, the powerful Martini. "Gosh, that's certainly a drink," his friend Leiter (who was drinking Scotch) said with awe. The drink was, of course, an individual Martini, too—his own invention. The tough side of the fourth ambiguity therefore converges with one side of the third: the Martini is tough and individual. Bond often drank in company, but his drinks, including his Martinis, were not fundamentally communal in spirit but rather an adjunct to a loner's existence. He was hardly a social creature. He was 007, licensed to kill, living outside the norms and patterns of everyday life and ordinary society. His Martini, even if he drank it with Leiter or M. or Solitaire or Tiffany Case—and he did drink it with all of them—was really the isolating Martini.[20] In the case of the women, one feels that it was not so much the Martini-of-the-relationship as a means by which Bond could briefly share his isolation. Bond's Martini, which is the isolating and fundamentally uncivilized Martini, demonstrates another, and the final, convergence: the Martini is uncivilized and individual and tough.

The use of two Englishmen, James Bond and W. S. Maugham, to illustrate the fourth ambiguity of the Martini, which is here analyzed as an aspect of American civilization, does not require special pleading. Maugham's ritualism was invented and refined in the United States. As for Bond, he belongs to a type that was already established in the 1930s in the American detective novel and movie. A good example is Dashiell Hammett's creation, Nick Charles. He is the suave-rough, urbane-rugged "private eye." The contrary qualities are reflected in his fictional biography. Formerly of the world of cops and robbers in New York City, he has gone to the West Coast and married the wealthy Nora. In the movie *The Thin Man* he boasts to his old pals in New York, "I am a gentleman now." Although the novel of the same name did not mention the Martini, the movie used this cocktail as a way of expressing one side of Nick Charles.[21] When he first appears on the screen, he is giving the bartender at the Normandie Hotel instructions on how to make a Martini. It should, he says, be shaken to a waltz; the Manhattan, however, to a foxtrot, and the Bronx to a two-step. He associates the Martini with the dance of the slowest rhythm and the most graceful and romantic mood. The Martini thus stands for Nick's gentler side; later we shall see him attack a pistol-wielding thug. The type, then, complete with Martini, long antedates James Bond, and is American.[22]

Dr. Lolli, who wrote admirably on social drinking when he was not writing as a medical researcher, sums up the ambiguity:

> The graceful, long-stemmed and glittering glass; the cool and colorless transparency of the fluid sketching the curves of a pitted olive or the floating irregularities of a lemon peel convey the impression of a powerful stillness, apt to affect with elegant explosiveness a person's body and mind. . . . The Latin name, a perhaps unconsciously motivated misnomer, connotes the sudden potentialities of a drink which may favor rapid shifts from the stillness of self-control to the impetuosity of passion.[23]

Still and powerful, elegant and explosive—these are forceful and refined formulations of the ambiguity under discussion.

THE LAST GOOD MARTINI, BY DANIEL HARDY

Nick sat against the wall at Harry's drinking his dry martini with courage and with grace. The way a dry martini at Harry's should be drunk. In the mirror that is placed behind bars so a man can tell when he is drinking too much he saw her pull open the door and enter and she was there. He had not seen Frances Barnes since the war. She was blond and had tawny skin and a lean unblighted face. Nick thought she was very beautiful.

"Hello, Nicholas Adams," she said.

"Hello, Barnes," Nick said. "Do you want a dry martini? You used to drink them beautifully. Waiter, *due martini*, with garlic olives, not the big ones."

The waiter brought the martinis and they touched edges.

"Here's to the short happy life, Frances," Nick said.

"Say, Nick, that was grand. I was going to say chin-chin."

"Thank you for not saying chin-chin, nor bottoms up."

Sensitive and tough

"You're welcome."

"Do you want to order dinner?" said Nick. "They still serve the big two-parted liver."

"Yes, thank you. That will be splendid," Frances said.

Ettore, with his emaciated face, came and took their orders and served them quickly and efficiently.

"What are you doing now, Nick? Still bowling?"

"Bowling well and writing well and other things are the only two important things in life," Nick said.

"I never understood why you really like to do this, this silliness of bowling."

Frances was beautiful but she was still dumb as hell, thought Nick. "The way to bowl," he said, "is for as long as you live against as long as a pin is standing in the lane. Do you remember George Tell?"

"Yes," said Frances. "He was a swell bowler. For Whom does Tell bowl now?"

"He bowls for my old man," Nick said. "He bowls straight and he bowls true but he still cannot hit a four-ten split with a handful of birdshot."

Frances laughed her good true laugh because of what she knew it did to him. He wanted to kiss her hard and well but he did not kiss her.

"And what have you been doing?" he asked.

"Still digging up stones and bones," she said. "I was looking for an alpine idol when I found this."

Frances took from her great huge bag a square stone covered with elaborate carvings. "What do you think?"

Nick looked across the liver and into the frieze and then remembered why his marriage to Frances Barnes had failed. Living with her had been like reading Sinclair Lewis before breakfast.

Frances finished her meal and rose to leave. "I don't suppose I will see you again," she said. It was a simple inquiry but Nick knew it meant the end of something. Nick said farewell to Barnes without regret as she turned and walked the other way from him.

"Ettore," he said, "put this nonsense on my bill."

Historical Background of the Ambiguities

THE QUESTION ARISES as to how the Martini became susceptible to such deep and pervasive ambiguity. The answer lies in the characteristics of its main ingredients, gin and vermouth. Both of these are oddities in American drinking, as appears both from comparison with other alcoholic beverages and from their history in the nineteenth century.

Gin and Vermouth Compared with Other Alcoholic Beverages

The principal distinction in American beverages is between alcoholic and nonalcoholic. The latter can be divided into coffee and tea, milk, soft drinks, fruit juices, and water. These all have their own cultural significance, and it would be interesting to discover which of them is (or are, if it is more than one) the opposite(s) of which alcoholic beverages. Roland Barthes has shown that in France, milk is the opposite of wine.[1] But what is the opposite of, say, beer in the United States?

Within the vast category of the alcoholic, the main distinction is between fermented and distilled beverages. In the United States, the principal—one is tempted to say the only—fermented beverages are wine and beer. The preeminence of this pair represents a historical disjunction in our alcoholic heritage, which divided itself millennia ago into the wine culture of the Mediterranean and southern Europe and the beer culture of northern Europe. Hard cider accounts for only a tiny percentage of the alcohol consumed each year in the United States. *Sake,* a sort of intermediate between beer and wine, is an oddity. Kumiss, fermented mare's milk, was marketed in this country for a short time in the early 1990s. It did not catch on.

But the invention of distillation was to bring an even more profound disjunction to Western civilization. The technique was discovered by Alexandrian Greeks in late antiquity and again, independently, by medieval Arab scientists, but neither used it to produce alcohol. The distillation of alcohol seems to have begun in Salerno in the first half of the twelfth century. Alcohol was at first only a medicine but was soon drunk for pleasure in the form of cordials or liqueurs. By the fourteenth century, primitive brandies were drunk all over Europe, though they did not entirely free themselves from the apothecaries and doctors until the seventeenth or eighteenth century.[2] Thereafter beer and wine were no longer opposites but belonged on the same side of the new cultural disjunction. The other side was distilled spirits.[3]

Today these spirits can be divided into two main types: spirits distilled directly from fermented mash in such a way that some of the distinctive flavor of the raw material is retained; and spirits made of highly "rectified" (i.e., purified) alcohol. To the first type belong the various brandies; cognac, distilled from wine; Scotch, principally from malted barley; bourbon, from corn and other grains; and rye, the namesake of its origin. The second type comprises the so-called white spirits, mainly gin, vodka, tequila, rum, schnapps, and aquavit, distilled from a wide variety of grains and plants. A "real" vodka would be distilled from potatoes, a "real" tequila from the heart of a cactus. Rum is from sugar cane. Of these, the most highly rectified or refined are gin and vodka. The others all contain at least a hint of the raw material from which they were born.

Gin is of two sorts, distinguished by the means by which the flavor is added to the spirits. In direct distillation, the vapors rise through a "gin head," a perforated container packed with juniper berries, herbs, and other aromatics. In redistillation, an already distilled spirit, flavorless and neutral, is revaporized and passes through a gin head. Distilled and redistilled gins differ from the other sort, which is called compound gin. This gin, as the name implies, is produced by adding the flavors, in the form of extracts, directly to the neutral spirits. This technique does not differ in principle from the bathtub gin of Prohibition. In either case, gin has to take a step backward, as it were, in the direction of the more flavorful white spirits, the brandies, and the whiskeys. If gin did not take this step, it would remain completely neutral in taste, utterly abstract. The flavor that is added to gin comes mainly from the juniper berries, and it is through the choice of the other contents of the gin head or the extracts in combined gin that one manufacturer differs from another. All, however, aim at something called dryness. When manufacturers of gin boast of the dryness of their product, they are not saying that it is not sweet—only a few special types of gin, for example, Hollands, are sweetened—but that it is as flavorless as possible while still retaining the characteristic taste of gin. The label on the Bombay Dry Gin bottle spoke of "that very slight, elusive flavor that makes Bombay a true, distinctive, dry Gin." In pursuing this goal of dryness, gin manufacturers inevitably lost the race to vodka, which is what gin would be if it had no flavor. The authors of an article on dry gins in *Consumer Reports* were quite right when they said that "the ultimate dry gin is vodka."[4] Paradoxically, it was the taste for dry gin that made the triumph of vodka inevitable.

Vodka is furthest removed from the substance (formerly potatoes) of its origin, and gin is next in neutrality. These two are the whitest spirits. They are literally the most refined. They are the most abstract, and therefore the most in need of definition. But of the two, gin, slightly more flavorful, is poorer in advertisable qualities. Vodka can point to its origins in the glorious days of pre-Soviet Russia. Gin, however, can offer itself only as a mixer, and that is why gin manufacturers continue to display the Martini and, in the summer, the gin and tonic or Tom Collins. Again, vodka can, by tradition, be drunk chilled and neat, as with caviar, but gin cannot. (Not in the United States in the twentieth century, that is. No doubt the wretches in "Gin Lane" drank it straight.) Only in virtue of its mixed state does gin attain an identity.[5]

The difference between gin and vodka, at least in advertisable qualities, is considerable, but the difference between gin and whiskey, beer, or wine is vast. All of these have some intrinsic character. Wine, pressed from grapes, is close to nature, close to the earth, and the very word "wine" is poetic. Beer is the thirst-quenching reward for the day's labor and is made from golden ingredients by master brewers. Whiskeys are handmade and then mellowed for years in wooden barrels. As for gin, no one quite knows what grain it has been distilled from. Aging is unnecessary. Only the flavoring sets one gin apart from another, and since gin is supposed to be as dry as possible, advertising will not say much about how it tastes. Since gin is the spirit without qualities, since its character is completely extrinsic, it can only be advertised as the essential ingredient in a mixed drink. Gin's only quality is privative: it lacks something, something with which it can be combined. "There are 108 ways the English keep dry with Gordon's," an advertisement once said.

What of vermouth? Where does it stand in relation to the other alcoholic beverages? In the scheme set out above, vermouth would seem to belong with wine, since wine is, or should be, its main constituent. But one will find almost nothing on vermouth in the vast literature of oenology. It is not even mentioned in most of the reference works in this field. Vermouth is not in fact a wine but at best a fortified wine and is properly neglected by the oenologist. I say "at best" for the reason that the wine from which vermouth is made is so highly clarified, the vermouth so complexly doctored, that it is not clear that the term "wine" is appropriate when this drink is under discussion. In any case, vermouth is fortified with neutral spirits and is therefore a crossbreed, like sherry and madeira. Unlike other fortified wines, however, vermouth—at least the dry variety—has never become popular in this country as a drink in its own right, despite occasional advertising campaigns. Dry vermouth is exactly like gin in requiring combination with something else, and most vermouth advertising has referred to the Manhattan and the Martini. In the first years after Prohibition, Martini and Rossi Vermouth was aimed exclusively at the drinkers of these cocktails, especially the Martini-drinker. An advertisement in *Life* in January 1935 began, "There are *three different* Martinis [i.e., cocktails]—be sure you try all three"—sweet, medium, and dry.

Dry vermouth and gin are both, then, oddities. Unlike the other alcoholic beverages, they are deficient in intrinsic character. The layman has little or no idea how dry vermouth is made or what it is, just as he neither knows nor cares—and indeed it makes no difference—what grain his gin is distilled from. (Good English gin is in fact distilled mainly from corn.) The combination in a Martini, however, of gin and vermouth, each of them relatively characterless, produces something as rich in significance as they are impoverished. The very blankness of gin and of vermouth by themselves is a surface on which all the ambiguity of the Martini can be inscribed.

Although the characterlessness of gin and of vermouth explains why the Martini had the potential for such elaborate significance, it does not explain why the Martini attracted the particular messages and ambiguities that have come to light. This question is far more difficult to answer, and answers probably should be sought in the still largely unknown history of gin and of vermouth in nineteenth-century America.

Gin in the United States

Although jenever, a species of gin, came to this country with the first Dutch settlers, the United States was never a gin-drinking country until the twentieth century. In the seventeenth and the first part of the eighteenth centuries, brandy was the main drink. On the Eastern seaboard, it was peach brandy in the South and as far north as Pennsylvania. Above that state, it was apple brandy or applejack. Rum took over in the course of the eighteenth century as the common man's drink, as the principal medium of exchange in the slave trade, and in bartering with the Indians. On the frontier, where rum was unavailable, they made whiskey—for both pleasure and profit. Grain could be shipped more economically in the form of distilled spirits than in the raw state. Home-distilling on the frontier in the eighteenth century culminated in the Whiskey Rebellion of 1791–94, the settlers' response to the federal government's attempt to impose taxes.[6]

Gin never established itself until the twentieth century, and a social history of gin in the United States would be half or a third as long as Gerald Carson's magnificent *The Social History of Bourbon*.[7] The progress of gin in this country may have been impeded by the bad reputation that it got from its abuse in England, but probably it was simply unable to find a place in the already packed national menu of alcohol. It has often been said that it was Prohibition that finally made us a gin-drinking nation. An article in *Scientific American*, March 1934, the year after Repeal, stated that "Prohibition . . . lifted gin out from the shady and somewhat disreputable regard in which it was held before the dry era and made it fashionable. Tipplers who once disdained it, save in an occasional cocktail, not only learned to drink it, but actually to make it."[8] Some of those who learned to make gin preferred their own product to what they could buy legally when Repeal came. Kenneth Roberts contributed a Martini recipe to *So Red the Nose, or Breath in the Afternoon* (1935) and included instructions for making gin, with the comment, "My one eccentricity is thinking that homemade gin is better than the purchased variety."[9]

One can get a sense of the relative popularity of gin and whiskey at the end of the nineteenth century from *Mida's National Register of Trade Marks*.[10] At that time, when production was far more localized than it is now, trademarks numbered 1,599 for whiskey and 64 for gin. What F. R. Stewart wrote in *American Ways of Life* seems true: "During most of the history of the United States the drinking of gin has been considered almost a depravity and the drinking of straight gin might be so considered even today."[11] Little did he know that a gin company would be advertising "the naked Martini" (i.e., straight gin) only a few years after he wrote these words. But his sense of gin's place in the history of American drinking is surely correct and is borne out by what is known of the Gin Cocktail, the forerunner of the Martini.

The Cocktail

The Gin Cocktail prompts a brief digression on the history of the cocktail. This kind of drink was invented at the turn of the eighteenth century and was defined in the *Hudson (New York) Balance* on May 13, 1806, thus: "*Cock tail*, then, is a stimulating liquor, composed of spirits of any kind, *sugar, water,* and *bitters*—it is vulgarly called *Bittered sling*."[12] The sling was a drink composed of roughly equal parts of spirits and sweetened water. Bitters, then, were the differential ingredient that created the cocktail. This point was made to Henry Didimus, a visitor to New

Orleans in 1835–36. He recounts drinking a brandy cocktail and asking how it differed from a brandy toddy. He was told:

> Now the difference between a brandy-cocktail and brandy-toddy is this: a brandy-toddy is made by adding together a little water, a little sugar, and a great deal of brandy—mix well and drink. A brandy cocktail is composed of the same ingredients, with the addition of a shade of Stoughton's bitters; so that the bitters draw the line of demarcation.[13]

In New Orleans, then, the cocktail might have been called a bittered toddy. A toddy was, of course, about the same thing as a sling. Bitters are again what makes the drink, transforming the eighteenth-century toddy into something new.

The origin of the cocktail and the etymology of the name are unknown, although many conjectures are strewn about in the literature on this subject.[14] The use of this drink, however, is fairly clear. Jerry Thomas states in his recipe book of 1862, *How to Mix Drinks, or The Bon Vivant's Companion*, "The 'Cocktail' is a modern invention, and is generally used on fishing and other sporting parties, although some *patients* insist that it is good in the morning as a tonic."[15] One finds a similar statement in William Terrington's *Cooling Cups and Dainty Drinks* (1869): "Cocktails are compounds very much used by 'early birds' to fortify the inner man."[16]

In the South in the nineteenth century, drinkers were divided into "slingers" and "eleveners." The former took the first drink of the day immediately upon waking. The latter, who were considered weaklings, did not imbibe until eleven o'clock in the morning.[17] Foreign travelers in the United States were aghast at the amounts of alcohol consumed, and at the practice of drinking before breakfast. Sir William Howard Russell wrote in *My Diary North and South* (1863):

> In the matter of drinks, how hospitable the Americans are! I was asked to take as many as would have rendered me incapable of drinking again; my excuse on the plea of inability to grapple with cocktails and the like before breakfast, was heard with surprise, and I was earnestly entreated to abandon so bad a habit.[18]

In the same year in which Sir William published his diary, Henry Porter and George Roberts defined the English position on cocktails in *Cups and Their Customs*:

> For the "sensation-drinks" which have lately travelled across the Atlantic we have no friendly feeling; they are far too closely allied to the morning dram, with its thousand verbal mystifications, to please our taste; and the source from which eye-openers and "smashers" come, is one too notorious for un-English behaviour to be welcomed by any man who deserves

well of his country: so we will pass the American Bar, with its bad brandies and fiery wine, and express our gratification at the slight success which "Pick-me-up," "Corpse-reviver," "Chain-lightning," and the like, have had in this country.[19]

But in 1880 Leo Engel, who kept an "American Bar" in London, began one of his advertisements, "Try a cocktail in the morning."[20]

The nineteenth-century cocktail was, then, a morning drink and traded somewhat on bitters' reputation as a good stomachic. (Similarly, gin is said to have gained a higher social acceptance in England when naval officers used it to dilute the angostura they drank as a specific for fever. The same application of gin to quinine led to the gin and tonic.) The cocktail was also drunk in the out-of-doors. Its social standing was either high- or low- but not middle-class, as the use of the Gin Cocktail in the nineteenth century will show.

The earliest references to this cocktail that I could find occurred in Boston newspapers in June 1838, apropos of a mock battle staged by two French warships, L'Hercule and La Favourite, off Newport, Rhode Island. The drink was already well enough known to be abbreviated g.c. The author of an unsigned article in the Boston Morning Post, who went to see the mock battle, told of taking an early train to Providence and then boarding a boat: "The boat was to start at 9; we had about ten minutes grace, and went down to the forward cabin, where the Drab Beaver and the younger [his traveling companions] imbibed a g.c. each, and I took a p.g.s. [pretty good snort?]."[21]

In the Columbian Sentinel, in a column of quotations from other newspapers, another journalist who attended the mock battle is mentioned. He was a passenger on the Richmond, another of the boats that carried spectators: "Among the editorial fraternity who came in the J. W. Richmond, we noticed our venerable friend, Major Russell, formerly of the Boston Centinel.—N. Y. Whig." The editors of the Columbian Sentinel comment: "The Major was in excellent spirits, and the youngest man on board the boat. He was refreshed with a G.C. on the passage."[22]

These references to the g.c. or G.C. give a sense of the sort of men who favored the drink. The anonymous author of the article in the Boston Morning Post is a wit and a sophisticate. The tone of the editors' comment in the Columbian Sentinel is, I should think, jocular and worldly.

But the Gin Cocktail was the drink not only of journalists but also of frontiersmen, as one can learn from the play Madmen All, or The Cure of Love published in 1847. The protagonist is Sam Markham, a Philadelphian, who is the rival of Huskisson Hodgson, an Englishman, for the affections of Garafelia Fizgig. Phil Peters is a friend of Sam's from New York. In the scene in which the Gin Cocktail is mentioned, Phil and

Historical Background

Sam are baiting the Englishman. Phil, whom the Englishman is meeting for the first time, pretends to be a "frank Western man":

HODG. Auh—Mr. Bragg [Phil's pseudonym]—auh—do you drink much malt liquor in your pawts—auh—I have a brothaw—auh—that is—yes—yaas—

PHIL. Look here, *stranger,* why don't you speak as if you warn't afraid o' what you was sayin', instead o' coughin' like an old steamboat—puff—auh—puff—auh—puff—auh? Speak out like a ringed pig.

HODG. I merely ausked if you drank much malt liquor in your pawts.

PHIL. Do we drink spring water? No sir: we drink Tom and Jerrys some—gin-cocktails putty considerable—but mostly stone fence [a mixture of cider and whiskey] barefooted![23]

So the Gin Cocktail typifies the uncouthness of the American frontier.

Two of these drinks appear again in a satirical article on "Pithole" (Pittsburgh) in the *Nation,* September 21, 1865. The author describes the sounds he hears upon entering his hotel: "Tinkling glasses show that the versatile whiskey is transforming itself into brandy smashes, gin cocktails, Tom-and-Jerrys, and other spirit-stirring potations."[24] These drinks are aspects of the general depravity of Pittsburgh.

The Gin Cocktail, then, stood both high and low. It was the drink of the urban sophisticate and of the frontiersman. The father of the Martini thus had the same characteristics as the son: it was both civilized and uncivilized and, one might venture to say, both sensitive and tough. But the invention of the Martini presupposes vermouth.

Vermouth in the United States

The first shipment of French, and thus dry, vermouth to the United States was carried by the *Clairborn* under the command of Captain Charles Warham in 1851. The amount was one hundred cases. The destination was New Orleans. My source for these facts is a copy of the bill of lading sent me by the Etablissements Noilly Prat & Cie. Martini and Rossi claims to have exported their vermouth, which was sweet, in 1834, but I could not obtain documentation or any historical information from the Italians.[25]

Vermouth was not an instant success. In 1857 the liquor dealers C.J. Edward and Company of New York City remarked in the course of a long letter to the firm of Noilly Prat:

Nous ne pouvons rien vous dire du Vermouth car cet article est entière-ment inconnu sur notre marché. Mais il arrive souvent que de nombreux articles rendent bien ici, car les américains prennent aisément goût à tout ce qui est nouveau. Nous vous proposons donc de nous adresser 10 Caisses que nous nous efforcerons d'introduire dans la consommation et de faire connaître par le moyen des Droguistes et des Apothicaires.

[We can tell you nothing about vermouth because this article is completely unknown in our market. But it often happens that numerous articles sell well here, because Americans easily form a taste for anything that is new. We ask you, then, to send us ten cases, which we shall attempt to introduce into usage and to make known through druggists and apothecaries.]

The pioneers of vermouth were successful by the end of the century. At that time Noilly Prat was shipping twenty-five thousand cases a year to the United States, and by 1910 the figure had tripled.

Perusal of the recipe books that followed in the wake of Jerry Thomas's effort of 1862 suggests that it was in the 1880s that vermouth caught on, although I confess that I have not seen a single such book from the 1870s. In 1892, vermouth is rife in The Only William's *The Flowing Bowl,* and by 1898 the anonymous author of a tiny leatherbound manual of cocktails could state in his preface, "The addition of Vermouth was the first move toward the blending of cocktails and was the initial feature that led to their popularity."[26] This statement is historically shortsighted. The differential ingredient of a cocktail was bitters. But the author is probably right about vermouth's contribution to the popularity of cocktails. The addition of vermouth to the Gin Cocktail, at any rate, produced the premier American cocktail, the Martini.

The Origin and Destiny of the Martini

The recipe for the Gin Cocktail in Jerry Thomas's manual of 1862 (which does not contain a recipe for the Martini) is this:

3 or 4 dashes of gum syrup
2 do. bitters (Bogart's)
1 wine-glass of gin
1 or 2 dashes of curaçao
1 small piece-lemon peel; fill one-third full of fine ice;
    shake well, strain in a glass[27]

This recipe, with only minute divergences, appears in all the nineteenth-century manuals and persists into the beginning of the twentieth century. With the Gin Cocktail, compare the earliest recipe for the Martini I have found, that given by O. H. Byron in 1884:

2 dashes curaçao
2   "   Angostura bitters
½ wine-glass gin
½   "   Italian vermouth[28]

This is not a verbatim quotation. What I have done is to substitute gin for whiskey in Byron's Manhattan recipe, as he directs. The Martini, he says, is "same as Manhattan, only you substitute gin for whisky."

If one compares the two recipes just quoted, the earliest Martini appears to have been a Gin Cocktail minus syrup plus vermouth, and I believe that this is the correct historical description of the origin of the Martini. From another point of view, the bartender's, the Martini is a Manhattan made with gin. The two cocktails are often listed next to each other in the manuals. Sometimes one finds the Manhattan but not the Martini, as in the authoritative book by The Only William, where one might have expected to find the Martini, too.

Byron's instructions imply that there were both sweet and dry Martinis, corresponding to the two Manhattan recipes that he gives, one of which calls for Italian, the other for French, vermouth. He does not indicate in which Manhattan recipe you substitute gin for whiskey. I assume that he intended the sweet Manhattan as the model for the Martini, because there is nothing resembling a dry Martini in the nineteenth-century literature of mixology. For example, in 1895 George J. Kappeler gave not only a sweet and a dry but also an extra-dry Manhattan, which called for French vermouth. There was only one Martini, however, and it was sweet, made with Italian vermouth.[29] The generalization by "Cocktail" Boothby (William T. Boothby) holds good for the nineteenth-century Martini. He introduces his recipe for the Martini thus: "This popular appetizer is made without sweetening of any description, as the Old Tom Cordial gin and Italian vermouth of which it is composed are both sweet enough."[30]

What Boothby had in mind was the omission of gum or sugar syrup, that staple of early cocktails.[31] It is absent, as it happens, from Byron's Martini recipe, quoted above, but occurs in most of the others. Syrup was called for in the Martini recipe published by Jerry Thomas in the 1887 edition of his book;[32] by Harry Johnson (1888);[33] by Harry W. Stiles (1888), who, however, cautioned, "½ usual amount of syrup for cocktail";[34] by Henry J. Wehman (1891);[35] and later, despite Boothby, C. F. Lawlor (1895)[36] and Thomas Stuart (1896)[37] wanted gum syrup in their Martinis. But the decade of the 1890s saw the first glimmering of dryness, as Boothby's words imply. The syrup has disappeared from the Martini recipes published by Ranhofer (1893),[38] Kappeler (1895),[39] Joseph L. Haywood (1898),[40] anonymous (1898),[41] Frederic L. Knowles (1900),[42] and Tim Daly (1903),[43] although their Martinis were still sweet. They still used sweet gin and sweet vermouth.[44]

Up to this point I have concealed one of the great problems in the early history of the Martini and that is variance in nomenclature. In the preceding paragraphs, I used "Martini" to simplify the account.

« FIGURE 6 »
Martine cocktail.
Glass on left is not a Martini on the rocks but a mixing glass.
From Harry Johnson, New and Improved Illustrated Bartender's Manual,
or How to Mix Drinks of the Present Style *(New York, 1888)*

O. H. Byron, however, was in fact talking about a "Martinez." That was in 1884. So also in the 1887 edition of Jerry Thomas it was "Martinez."[45] "Martini" appears for the first time, so far as I know, in Harry Johnson's manual of 1888. (There is an earlier edition of 1881 that I have not been able to find.) But in the gruesome plate in this manual illustrating the Martini, it is called a Martine (Figure 6). One would have been tempted to consider this a misspelling if "Martine" did not also turn up in Charles Ranhofer's *The Epicurean* (1893). Was there, then, another name for the drink, pronounced "mar-teen"? In any case, "Martine" is never heard of again, and "Martini" and "Martinez" compete for the ascendancy. "Martinez" appears in Lawlor (1895), Stuart (1896), and Paul E. Lowe (1904),[46] but already by the time of Lowe, "Martinez" is simply being copied out of earlier books, and one doubts that it was a living name. "Martini," the name that, as we know, won out, appears in Wehman (1891), Kappeler (1895), Haywood (1898), anonymous (1898), Knowles (1900), and Daly (1903). Since Daly was the barman at the Parker House in Boston, the name "Martini" must have been in use in that city. When one considers that O. Henry mentions a "ready-made Martini" in a story set in the remote village of Mountain Valley, Georgia, in *The Gentle Grafter* of 1904, one concludes that "Martini" was ubiquitous in the United States by the turn of the century.[47]

I know less about nomenclature in England. The American Leo Engel, who published *American and Other Drinks* in London in 1880, mentions neither the Martinez nor the Martini. That is not surprising, since he cribbed nearly everything from the 1862 edition of Jerry Thomas, in which this drink did not appear. At the 1887 American Exposition in London, American Bartenders showed their inventiveness by serving a different cocktail on every day of the year except Sundays. On Saturday, March 5 of that year, the drink was "Gin and Vermouth."[48] Does this name mean that "Martinez" and "Martini" were not yet established, or that they would have been meaningless in England? Or that the English had already begun to speak of "Gin and It" and "Gin and French," so that "Gin and Vermouth" was a concession to their practice?

The name "Martinez" was the basis for a story about the origin of the Martini, which is retailed in such places as *The Book of Lists* and *The American Heritage Cookbook*. It once appeared in a Beefeater advertisement, too. This story has it that Jerry Thomas mixed the first Martinez in 1862 for a traveler on his way from San Francisco to Martinez, California. The date is taken from the first edition of Jerry Thomas's book, although this edition does not mention the Martinez; the Martinez, to repeat, was published for the first time by Byron, in New York in 1884. The function of the traveler in this story is to link two facts: one, that there exists a town called Martinez, twenty-six miles north of San Francisco; two, that Jerry Thomas, who worked in San Francisco, published a recipe—never mind the date—for a drink called Martinez.

The traveler's direction can, of course, be reversed. In Martinez, they believe that he was heading for San Francisco and that the drink was first mixed in *their* town. In 1965 Mrs. Nina MacLeod Ritch of Martinez gave a story about the cocktail to a columnist called The Knave who wrote for the *Oakland Tribune*. Mrs. Ritch gave him the facts as they had been given her by the fire chief of Martinez, Mr. John M. ("Toddy") Briones, when he was ninety-one. The Martinez, it turned out, was invented by Toddy's brother-in-law, Julio Richelieu, at Julio's bar on Ferry Street in Martinez. Now comes the traveler. A miner on his way to San Francisco stopped in at Julio's, ordered a drink, and paid for it with a gold nugget. Instead of change, he asked for something special. Julio mixed him up the first Martinez cocktail.[49]

This sort of origin story was parodied as early as 1912 by Kendall Banning in *The Squire's Recipes*. The recipes in this slim volume are for all the popular drinks of Banning's day, but each one is preceded by an account of how the eighteenth-century squire had invented and named it. The names are, of course, all suitably archaic. The Martini is the "Dartmouth Drachm," and this is how it was invented:

> During the winter of 1774, while the Squire was journeying from Boston Town to Dartmouth College on a matter not wholly unconnected with

business, he tarried for the night at the Tally-Ho Inn. Before the hearth in the tap room he fell in with a gentleman who had but just returned from Spain, bringing with him, from an ancient monastary [sic], a sweet, aromatic liqueur, which the monks made from divers blossoms and herbs after a secret process. With the connivance of the Squire, who mixed this sweet with other liquors, a pleasing quaff was obtained, but of such passing potency that all who partook were straightway much inspired. Upon learning that his companion was of the household of the Earl of Dartmouth, and would journey by the same coach on the morrow, the Squire forthwith christened the concoction the Dartmouth Drachm.[50]

The mysterious liqueur here is Benedictine; but the other ingredients are gin and vermouth. The squire was going in for that doctoring of the Martini that I discussed under the "personal" Martini (Ambiguity 3), but a Martini it clearly is, and it is made for a traveler and named after his destination. The resemblance of this story to the Martinez one is not, one suspects, fortuitous.[51]

To return to the problem of "Martini" and "Martinez," it is sometimes said that the former is a phonetic deformation of the latter, that if you say "Martinez" often enough it will turn into "Martini." That is not true. Nor is it possible that "Martini" arose as a "folk etymology" from "Martinez," like "planter's wart" from "plantar wart." Such an origin would presuppose that the name "Martini" was much more common and made sense when "Martinez" did not. They were simply two different names for the same thing, and we read in Stiles's manual, published in Chicago in 1888, that the Martinez was also called the Turf Cocktail and the Brighton.[52] To complicate matters, two other Martini-like cocktails had names of their own.

These two are of special interest because they appear to be the first dry Martinis. In 1896 Thomas Stuart, in a manual published in New York, gives the same directions for the Martinez that had been given by Byron in 1884; but in the last section of his book, called "New and Up-to-Date Drinks," Stuart presents the Marguerite Cocktail:

  1 dash of orange bitters
  2/3 Plymouth gin
  1/3 French vermouth.[53]

Plymouth gin, unlike the Old Tom gin of the nineteenth-century Martini, was not sweet. (It was distinguished by its intense aromatic flavor from London gin.) French vermouth was dry. Orange bitters were a regular ingredient in what was later called the dry Martini. The Marguerite appears again in the anonymous *Cocktails: How to Make Them* published in Providence in 1898. The context is revealing. The author gives recipes for the dry and extra-dry Manhattans, then the Marguerite, which corresponds with his extra-dry Manhattan, and then his two Martini recipes. Whereas in earlier manuals the Martini or Martinez was the "same as [the] Manhattan, only you substitute gin," now the Marguerite has inserted itself as the counterpart of the extra-dry Manhattan.

But the name "Marguerite" never caught on, probably because the Martini—drink and name—was already established by the end of the nineteenth century, and it was easier to call for a dry Martini. The Martini itself had already shown an incipient dryness at the beginning of the 1890s—it had already sensed its destiny. When the Martini turned dry, it was the same thing as the Marguerite and easily displaced this name (which was later applied to another drink, one that contained lime juice and the white of an egg).

The other name that should be mentioned in connection with the origin of the dry Martini is the Puritan Cocktail. In *The Cocktail Book: A Sideboard Manual for Gentlemen,* published in Boston in 1900, Frederic L. Knowles lists two Martini recipes (one of them calling for a teaspoonful of sherry) after his Manhattan recipes, just as one would expect. The Marguerite is absent, but he gives a Marguerite-like drink, called the Puritan Cocktail: "Three dashes orange bitters; one spoonful yellow chartreuse; two-thirds Plymouth gin; one-third French vermouth. Fill with ice, mix, and strain into a cocktail glass." It is the Marguerite plus one spoonful of yellow chartreuse. Why was it called Puritan? Because of its relative dryness, I should think. Both of Knowles's Martinis were made with sweet Old Tom gin and sweet Italian vermouth. His Puritan comes close to being a dry Martini, and the name is suggestive. Was the name chosen because of the drink's austerity? Compare the moral qualities that Donald G. Smith found in the drink (Simple Message 7) and Bassett's austere Martini (Ambiguity 1).

In the end, it must be admitted that no one knows who made the first Martini. The origins of the names "Martini," "Martinez," "Martine" (if that is a separate name and not a misspelling), and "Marguerite" are unknown. It is sometimes said that the Martini Cocktail is named after Martini and Rossi Vermouth or after the Martini-Henry rifle, but evidence for these etymologies is completely lacking. As for the date of origin, the drink must have been invented during the 1870s in order to gain enough currency to be mentioned in Byron's manual of 1884. Mason Hammond, professor of Latin emeritus at Harvard, told me in 1978 that his father, who graduated from Harvard in 1881, was drinking Martinis as an undergraduate. William F. Mulhall, who went to work as a bartender in the Hoffmann House in New York in 1882, later recalled the Martini as one of the "famous cocktails" that he served there.[54]

The destiny of the Martini is easier to grasp than its early history.

What Aristotle said of Greek tragedy in the *Poetics* is also true of the Martini: "Having passed through many changes, it found its natural form, and there it stopped." Two aspects of the Martini's natural form had already been discovered by the time of the Marguerite: coldness and dryness. The dryness may seem questionable, since the proportions were only 2:1; but I am not arguing that there is a natural recipe for the Martini, a natural proportion of gin to vermouth. I am arguing that there is a natural form, which comprises the essential qualities of the Martini. In any case, the difference that the proportion makes is not as great as it seems. The difference between 3:1, the greatest strength attained by the prewar Martini, and the supposedly mighty 7:1 of later decades, is in fact negligible. The 7:1 Martini contains only 3 percent more alcohol.[55]

Coldness and dryness are two aspects of the natural form of the Martini. A third is clarity, which is already in the nature of gin. The marvelous clarity of the Martini that we see in gin advertisements, clarity as of a gelid mountain stream, belongs to what I am calling the natural form of the Martini. If gins were once yellowish, it was because of the barrels they were shipped (not aged) in, and yellow tint was artificially added to some gins to suggest aging that gin does not require and does not receive. The vermouth was probably what always made Martinis yellow or amber up until some point in perhaps the late 1930s, when dry vermouth became clear.[56] The chartreuse, absinthe, and orange bitters that were added to the Martinis of the 1930s would also have given the drink a yellowish cast.

In order to make their contribution to the Martini's clarity, manufacturers of dry vermouth submit their product to hot and cold stabilization. Refrigeration precipitates substances that would form a deposit in the bottle. Pasteurization kills microorganisms and causes other organic substances to coagulate. They can then be removed by a fine, sterilizing filtration. The intent of these final steps in the production of vermouth is to make it colorless. Once again, vermouth shares a prime characteristic with gin: clarity.[57]

The fourth aspect of the form of the Martini is purity. This aspect is already given in clarity and dryness, but not entirely. The purity of the Martini is also active and exclusive. It wards off contamination; and DeVoto said of the Martini-rite, "The goal is purification."[58] As I have already said, the Martini resists the intrusion of personality, while permitting each drinker to believe that it is his or her own private creation. The traditional garnishes of the Martini—the olive, the lemon peel, and the onion ("Gibson" is another name, not another drink)—have been merely decorative and have only set off the purity of the drink.[59] Other garnishes must be equally restrained, simply because of the nature of the drink. The role of the garnish is to be "the other," to be something coarser, more palpable, that by contrast reveals the Martini in its ethereal purity.

The classic Martini glass also contributes to the Martini's purity. The drinker holds the glass by the stem. This custom has the practical advantage of separating the warmth of the hand from the desired coldness of the bowl, but the purpose of the custom is not fundamentally practical. Just as the glass must be clear, to reveal the pure color, or colorlessness, of the drink, the glass is stemmed in order symbolically to elevate its contents. The very impracticality of the stem, which makes the glass easier to upset and easier to break when it is upset, lifts the Martini above the dull defilement of the everyday and contributes to what an advertisement for Beefeater Gin called "the clean taste."

The form of the Martini, consists, then, of coldness, dryness, clarity, and purity. It is a simple, strict, one might say puritanical, drink. Its pleasure, which is not voluptuous but astringent, can only be expressed by oxymoron: sensuous coldness, opulent dryness, mysterious clarity, alluring purity.

Although gin and vermouth are each highly refined, highly artificial, although they are combined to create the Martini, this drink seems to come back to the radical purity of the simplest element, water. The Martini should look like a glass of water, though not water as we usually encounter it but a more lucent, crystalline water. In the Middle Ages the marvel of distillation was expressed in the name given one of the first spirits, *aqua vitae*, water of life. In its day this name must have been heard as a play on *panis vitae*, bread of life, though it somehow avoided the suspicion of impiety. In the medieval Latin Bible, Jesus said, "*Ego sum panis vitae*" (I am the bread of life) (John 6:35, 48); and in the Eucharist the bread is his body. Distilled alcohol, as *aqua vitae*, was, then, a secular sacrament, a counterpart to both the bread and the wine, those earthy elements that provoked centuries of theological debate about their material status in the Holy Communion. Distilled alcohol could appear as already transubstantiated, already "spirit," to use another of its early names. It was an elixir that carried the promise of everlasting youth, immortality on earth. An early treatise on its properties was entitled *La conservation de la jeunesse* (by Arnaud de Villeneuve, before 1313).[60] The Martini, capturing, as no other cocktail, the look of the "water of life" and functioning as a sacrament in its own ritual, holds this promise for postmedieval drinkers.

But in another religious context, danger arises from this purity. In Greek myth the encounters of humans with the god Dionysus brought them not life but violent death. One should not attempt to meet alcohol face to face, though the Martini-drinker wants to flirt with such a confrontation, with the unmediated, unalloyed joy of alcohol itself. It is easy to see why one of the typical Martini-drinkers is a certain kind of loner or an alcoholic. This type is engaged in a struggle, or, if he is lucky, in only a séance, with alcohol itself. He comes to know the darkness of the Martini, a drink so refined and civilized that it can be barbaric, so white and clear that it can be black.

The Secular Sacrament: The Rite of the Martini

The Martini-rite was originally in the hands of bartenders. They were the ones who mixed the first Martinis, and men drank them in saloons and clubs. These bartenders were priests too, and in one's attendance upon their mixing of one's drink one was entering the sacred circle of good fellowship and good cheer. A bit of doggerel from the turn of the century, called "The Great American Cocktail," concludes, "a cher confrère you are / If you admire the cocktail they pass across the bar."[61] The camaraderie of the bar was missed in the old Waldorf, and this deficiency was made good by the addition of the Astoria in 1897. Its bar became a world-famous meeting place. A. S. Crockett, in his history of the Waldorf-Astoria, speaks eloquently of the traditional mahogany counter and brass rail: men "much preferred to receive their cocktails and highballs direct from the hands of the barman. . . . It was a good old American custom, and eyeing a cocktail in the making was watching a rite."[62] Such was the original Martini-rite, performed by the bartender, by which the drinker entered the circle of chers confrères.

The rite of the middle-class Martini could not come into existence until drinking had moved into the home, until there was a "saloon in the home," to use the title of a recipe book published in 1930.[63] This rite also required that every man be his own bartender. Traditionally, however, men did not know how to mix drinks. This skill was never acquired, for example, by Jack London, a Martini-drinker like his Burning Daylight. When London became prosperous, he moved to a farm in Valley of the Moon (his name for the Sonoma Valley) and had his cocktails shipped to him in bulk from a bar in Oakland.[64] London was not exceptionally ignorant. As long as men drank in bars and clubs, they were not likely to learn how to mix drinks, even if they liked to watch them being mixed. Although a score of bartender's manuals were published before the turn of the century, these were addressed to bartenders, not to the layman.

I believe that the general ignorance of mixology partly explains the origin of prepared, bottled cocktails. These were introduced by Heublein in 1892, and the company's advertising in the 1890s, which presupposes that drinking at home is something new, promises "a better cocktail at home than is served over any bar in the world."[65] Heublein's advertisements in epistolary form taught consumers that women drank cocktails at home—women of refinement and high social position. On March 15,

1894, "Honora" writes to a friend about a Vermouth Cocktail she has been drinking on the sly before breakfast: "What a bother it would have been to stop to make it, or to ring for one to be served, thus giving one's indecorous thirst away to the whole household!"[66]

Cocktails before dinner did not become customary until the 1910s, although I have found a reference to this use of cocktails as early as 1883,[67] and Martinis before dinner in the first decade of the twentieth century appeared in connection with Simple Messages 3 and 4. Drinking was driven into the home ultimately by the Volstead Act, which became law in 1920. The cocktail in England was in step with, or a few years behind, our own. Alec Waugh writes:

> When I started to go to dinner parties in 1919, the cocktail habit had not reached London. You were invited for 8 o'clock; you were welcomed by your host and hostess, you were introduced to the lady whom you were to "take in" to dinner, and you stood around. It was *le mauvais quart d'heure*—and very bad it could be on occasions, particularly for a young man of 21, as I was, not too sure of himself and anxious to make a good impression. The young of today are lucky to have been spared that experience. And even after the cocktail had made its first appearance in the more avant-garde circles, it was only one cocktail, and you had to drink it quickly if you arrived seven minutes late; if you were invited for 8, at a quarter past you went in to dinner. (Alec Waugh, *Wines and Spirits,* Time-Life Books)[68]

I heard something similar about the proto–cocktail hour in the United States when I was doing research for the first edition of this book in 1978. Mrs. Dorothy Wilson, an eighty-five-year-old resident of Cambridge, Massachusetts, recalled a dinner party at the Nieman home in Milwaukee that she attended with her parents when she was a child.[69] Upon entering the house, the grown-ups were served a very small Martini. They drank it in a matter of minutes, without hors d'oeuvres, and were immediately shown into the dining room. This was in about 1910. The Niemans, Mrs. Wilson told me, were considered avant-garde, and she remembered that it was especially shocking to see women drinking cocktails. Such a thirst was "indecorous," as "Honora" put it. Women might with propriety drink wine but nothing else alcoholic.

Franklin D. Roosevelt, who became president in 1933, the year of Repeal, the end of the Thirteen Years, was an exemplary Martini-ritualist. Although he was not a big drinker, he loved to mix Martinis and other cocktails, just as he loved to carve turkey for a large table of guests.[70] James Costigan, in *Eleanor and Franklin,* written for ABC television in 1977, justly depicted Roosevelt mixing "the first legal Martini."[71] Roosevelt would invite his secretaries and staff to an informal and light-hearted gathering at the end of the day, and he called this occasion "the children's hour," borrowing the expression from Ray Moley, who held a similar gathering for his assistants.[72] Roosevelt would sometimes quote Longfellow's lines:

Between the dark and the daylight,
When the night is beginning to lower,
Comes a pause in the day's occupations,
That is known as the Children's Hour.

Costigan had Roosevelt say, at the mixing of the first legal Martini, "Children, a tradition is born," and in fact such was Roosevelt's use of the White House, such was his dramatization of the presidency, that he gave the cocktail hour, and the Martini-rite in particular, an official sanction. He was the chief priest celebrating before the whole nation the same rite that each citizen would imitate in his private devotions. Roosevelt's silver cocktail cups are now preserved in the Franklin D. Roosevelt Library at Hyde Park (Figure 7).[73] Even before he took office, the tools of the rite had become common in American households. The cocktail set, consisting of glasses and shaker, was already in the 1920s a typical wedding gift (Figure 8).

In the course of time the Martini-rite came to be focused on the attainment of maximal dryness. The family circle, the guests, the men at the bar—these devotees of the Martini-cult no longer witnessed the magical transformation of gin and vermouth into the Martini. What they now saw was one trick or another by which the vermouth was kept away from the gin. The Martini glass or the mixing pitcher was rinsed with vermouth, which was then poured out before the addition of gin. This technique produced the "in-and-out Martini." Alternatively, the gin was poured into an empty vermouth bottle and then over ice. The fetishist of dryness might also pour the vermouth over ice cubes held in a sieve over the sink, and then pour the gin over the same ice cubes into a pitcher. If this technique imparted too strong a flavor of vermouth or excessive dilution of the gin, he might let the draft from an electric fan blow across the top of an open vermouth bottle in the direction of the pitcher or shaker. The proportion of vermouth to gin could be still further reduced if he placed the vermouth bottle next to the gin and turned the bottle slowly so that the label, with the word "vermouth," was exposed to the gin for perhaps a second. Since even this technique was considered risky, the fetishist might keep his vermouth in storage and merely whisper "vermouth" over the gin, or salute in the direction of France.[74]

These new forms of the Martini-rite were already practiced in the early 1950s. In 1952 C. B. Palmer, in an article called "The Consummately Dry Martini," thought that the decade might be called "the Numb (or

« FIGURE 7 »
FDR's cocktail shaker.
In this the high priest of the Martini-rite mixed the world's worst Martinis.
Photograph courtesy of The Franklin D. Roosevelt Library,
Hyde Park, N.Y.

Glazed) Fifties."[75] At about this time the vermouth atomizer came into use. It blew a mist of vermouth over the Martini glass. For some reason the various gadgets that succeeded the atomizer did not appear until the 1960s, although they too were for the sole sake of dryness. First came the plastic cubes to house the ice and prevent any meltage from diluting the gin. Then in the mid-1960s Hammacher Schlemmer introduced the vermouth dropper, a long, calibrated eyedropper designed to fit into a vermouth bottle (Figure 9). Mr. Ray Lyman of Lyman Metal Products invented the Martini scale, a device with a jigger for vermouth and a larger one for gin suspended at either end of a crossbeam that could be adjusted to secure proportions up to 25:1. From 1967 to 1970 Gorham offered the Martini spike, a finely calibrated syringe in a sterling silver

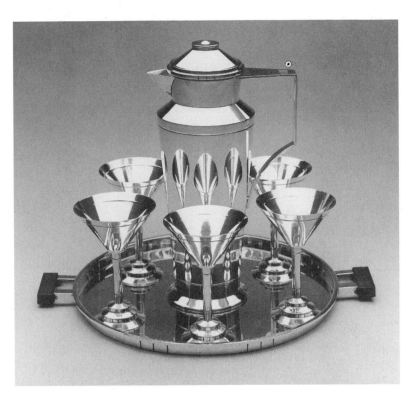

« FIGURE 8 »
Cocktail set by Erik Magnussen, 1929. Silver and Bakelite.
Height of shaker, 12 inches.
The Newark Museum/Art Resource, New York

casing, by which infinitesimal amounts of vermouth could be injected into a Martini (Figure 10). In the same period Mr. Fred Pool invented the Martini stones. These were marble stones to be soaked in vermouth and then placed in the gin. Mr. Pool told me that these stones were not mere gimmickry. They made the vermouth taste better by neutralizing its acid.

Coincidentally, the late 1960s also saw the advent of dry Martini–flavored candy (a violation of Simple Message 6). It was produced by John Wagner and Sons, Inc., of Ivyland, Pennsylvania. Mr. Ralph Starr, the president of the company, described the candy to me in a letter: "It is a non-alcoholic product, but we use the same essences and herbal flavors which are used in the production of gin, and hence arrive at the same basic flavor. . . . [It's] really quite surprising how close one can get." He sent me the cardboard container in which the candy is sold. It has a picture of an Eskimo pouring out a Martini for a polar bear as they sit

Historical Background

« FIGURE 9 »
The Vermouth dropper, by Invento, mid-1960s
Photograph courtesy of Hammacher Schlemmer

atop the entrance to an igloo. The polar bear rests a friendly paw on the Eskimo's shoulder. This is a Martini of friendship. The glasses are of the classic design.[76]

This candy, despite its name, was presumably sweet, but everything else connected with Martinis in the 1960s was devoted to dryness. Where the rite of dryness and its attendant gadgets left off, imagination took over. Nick's Restaurant in Boston claimed that its bartender had "succeeded in isolating the vermouth molecule" on August 16, 1963, at twelve noon, and issued a placard to this effect. The conceit was carried a step further by Mr. Paul A. Pollock of Lowell, Massachusetts, who wrote that at the time of the first atomic explosion at White Sands, New Mexico, a bottle of vermouth was secreted in the device and thus subjected to fission.[77] Thereafter Mr. Pollock and his friends could add vermouth to

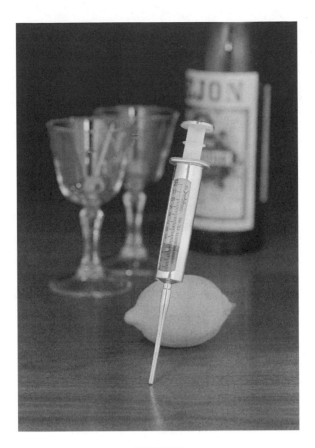

<< FIGURE 10 >>
The Martini spike, ca. 1967
*Photograph courtesy of the Gorham Division
of Textron*

their Martinis simply by holding their glasses out the window. This was the "fissionable Martini." The story was told of a mountain climber who mixed himself a Martini on the face of a peak in the Alps. He shouted "vermouth" in the direction of the neighboring mountains. When the echo came back, he held up his glass and in this way obtained a sufficient amount of vermouth.

The cult of dryness richly deserved the satire it received at the hands of Mr. Bertram Stanleigh in 1966. Then affiliated with the American Standards Association, he produced a short treatise called *Safety Code and Requirements for Dry Martinis* to commemorate the retirement of the company's managing director. This treatise parodied the technical style of the company's publications, with tables, diagrams, numbered paragraphs, subparagraphs, and sub-subparagraphs, and a sprinkling of useless footnotes. Although Stanleigh's work was reprinted and copy-righted in 1974 by what is now the American National Standards Institute, it remained an in-house joke, and was and is, regrettably, unavailable to the general public.

The butt of the satire is, of course, dryness, and to a lesser extent the related desire to get as much alcohol as possible into a single Martini. Table 1 is entitled "Maximum Permissible Olive Displacement." Table 2, "Proportions," shows 16:1 as the *lowest* permissible ratio of gin to vermouth, and the gin must be 100 proof. Paragraph 5.2.3 and Figure 2 explain the radiation method of mixing:

> A 60 watt incandescent lamp is placed on a flat surface 9 inches from a sealed bottle of vermouth. A sealed bottle of gin is placed on the other side of the bottle of vermouth at a distance of 23 inches. . . . The lamp may be illuminated for an interval of 7 to 16 seconds. The duration of exposure is governed by the color of the bottles.

Stanleigh's definition of "rocks" comes as no surprise: "The solid state of H_2O on which an American Standard dry martini is never served." And yet in 1966 it would already have been truer to say that the Martini was usually served on the rocks. With the Martini on the rocks, the Martini-rite, which had been usurped by the fetishism of dryness, finally died. When the Martini could be prepared by sloshing gin over ice cubes in a glass, with perhaps a dash of vermouth, ceremony was no longer required or even possible. The casualness of the Martini on the rocks obviously corresponds to many other changes in the social life of the 1960s, that decade of riots, assassinations, and war. In the history of the Martini, the Martini on the rocks represents the ultimate denial of the classic, civilized Martini and its rite, a denial already foreboded in the movement toward a "naked Martini," a Martini consisting of pure gin.

The Persistence of the Image

The demise of the Martini-rite might seem to represent an ineluctable historical incursion into what I have called a synchronous system. That is not the case. The system has remained intact. The executives of Seagram's who decided to spend vast sums of money on an advertisement that linked the Martini with the *sake* ceremony were not making a mistake.[78] The Martini is still in *belief,* if not in fact, the centerpiece of a rite, and people who would not drink straight gin on the rocks will drink straight gin on the rocks if it is called a Martini.

The contradictory relation of belief to actual practice is perfectly expressed in a Seagram's advertisement of 1979, which is a variant of the 1978 production, "THE SEAGRAM'S GIN MIDNIGHT MARTINI." More or less the same couple, in the same attitude, hold the classic stemmed

Martini glasses. But the caption beneath the couple reads, "For a Perfect Martini, just pour Seagram's Gin gently over the ice and forget the vermouth." The contradiction between the drink in the photograph and the drink prescribed in the caption shows how the traditional imagery of the Martini has maintained itself. To order "straight gin," which is what Seagram's is really recommending, would be, after all, an eccentricity.[79] But to order a "Martini," even if that is only a sobriquet for straight gin or vodka, is to become a *cher confrère*, a welcome guest, one of the family. The rite, in which all the communal virtue of the civilized Martini was expressed, is still alive in the imagination.

Conclusion

C LAES OLDENBURG'S *Tilting Neon Cocktail* (1983) is one of his "multiples"—that is, a work issued in multiple copies (Plate 5). There are fifty of the *Cocktail,* with number and signature engraved on the base.[1] At first glance the sculpture seems to repeat the well-established rhetoric of Pop Art. An object in the urban landscape, so familiar that it is almost invisible, is refabricated in industrial materials and by techniques that suggest that it too is or could be mass-produced. The object is already iconographic or symbolic—a target, a flag, a label or object with its label, a comic strip, or, as in this case, a sign. Then, unexpectedly, something rather glamorous emerges from this unlikely object and these "unartistic" techniques. So Oldenburg takes the ubiquitous neon cocktail sign and renders it in stainless steel, cast aluminum, acrylic paint, and Plexiglas, and produces a rather elegant Martini glass.

True Pop Art, its materials and its production, can be repeated. It is indeed a "multiple." The particular copy at which one is looking is only a single unit of production. There could be thousands more. In fact in this case it is one of fifty. This limit, which certainly does not belong to the visual effect of any particular copy, is still ultimately part of the effect. One has seen the neon sign everywhere (Plate 4), but one has not seen *Tilting Neon Cocktail* everywhere. One knows that even if it is repeatable, it has not in fact been repeated on a mass scale. It is a rare commodity. It is art.

To this extent the sculpture and the neon sign are simply different, and the former leaves the latter behind. Oldenburg the Pop Artist has done no more than an Old Master painting a still life. The fruit and the

97

bric-a-brac of the still life perished long ago, with no regret or even inter-est on our part. The painting is what matters. What about the neon sign that lies behind Oldenburg's sculpture? Looking again at *Tilting Neon Cocktail,* one begins to become aware of a rather complex dialogue between the sculpture and the original. Unlike the Old Master, Olden-burg does not want completely to replace his subject with his own work. The theme of the dialogue is already indicated in the word "tilting" in the sculpture's title. In Oldenburg's work, because it is three-dimen-sional, the tilt is more precarious, and it is accentuated by the elongated stem of the glass; and the fact that the sculpture can be revolved seems to reemphasize the sense of movement. In the neon sign, in two dimen-sions, the tilt is less threatening and is hardly noticed. After Oldenburg's *Cocktail,* it is noticed and begins to seem odd.

The tilt might signify various things. It might be just an attention-get-ting device, something like the scare quotes around a word. Or perhaps it says, "In this establishment, cocktail glasses are being tilted (i.e., cock-tails are being drunk)—come in and partake." Or the message might be even stronger: "This tilting glass is tipsy, as you will be if you come in and partake." In the last case the effect of drinking, tipsiness, to which the sign beckons is incorporated in the tilt of the sign itself, which is intended as the cause of the drinking. The sign would be the rhetorical figure of effect for cause. Or one could say that the signified (tipsiness) is brought back into the signifier (the neon sign). Oldenburg's own work prompts these reflections by restating the tilt of the sign, and he repeats, as it were, what he is saying by letting the viewer spin the sculpture. It is tipsy, and it can become dizzy.

Oldenburg reconstitutes in three dimensions the original that lies be-hind the sign, but he does so from the material provided by the sign itself. He even remains true to the technique of neon sign-making, which re-quires the bending of a continuous piece of glass tubing. He comments: "A rod of stainless steel, which has the look and feel of a 'white' liquor, like the vodka or gin of martinis, was substituted for the neon, and was formed, as neon must be, in a single, unbroken line." Oldenburg thus steps into the line of communication that goes from neon sign to po-tential customer and that leads to buying a drink inside the bar. Olden-burg interrupts this communication by consuming the sign itself. His consumption only leads to another sign, his sculpture. He establishes a short-circuit between the original and his own work.

But the original of the neon sign is itself, as my book has shown, al-ready a sign, an image, a symbol, and a highly complex one. There is no simple, essential original to be rebuilt, as Oldenburg well knows. With-out even drinking the drink, without much concern for particular mes-sages—though, as will soon appear, he has some concern—he shows that the consumption of the Martini is only the recirculation of meaning or meanings, whatever they may be in any particular instance. Oldenburg is the ultimate Martini drinker. The style of Pop Art and his own gifts are admirably suited to say something about the Martini that theoretical movements of the second half of the twentieth century have been saying about communication in general.

Oldenburg is not, however, only a consumer. He had intended to "serve" his cocktail to a rather select group in particular circumstances. He says:

> After the 1960s, fund-raising was nearly always the impetus for my multiple making. Fund-raising especially influenced the choice of subject for *Tilting Neon Cocktail*. I visualized the benefactors of The New Museum of Contemporary Art seated around a banquet table with a cocktail sculpture at each setting. In fact, I had wanted a motive for this ubiquitous subject since 1954 when I noticed that every bar in San Francisco was identified by an identical emblem, a cocktail glass in neon.
>
> This well-established sign for happy times is conventionally tilted as if the glass itself were intoxicated. . . . In three dimensions, this left parts of the subject, such as the walls of the glass and its contents, to the imagination, making the cocktail a rather abstract object. To bring the subject back from geometry to nature, the olive, cradled in the imaginary funnel of the glass and surrounded by the imaginary alcohol, is treated in a painterly way.
>
> There are overtones of the glistening black dance floors from the 1930s film musicals, or of the earliest plastic—Bakelite—in the curved corner fragment of a bar table, on which the *Tilting Neon Cocktail* can be revolved. But the envisioned choreography of an opulent table setting with sixty-five twirling cocktails never materialized.[2]

In the function in which Oldenburg had imagined it, the Martini of course would have conveyed some or all of the Simple Messages. It is unnecessary to point them out one by one in his statement. The guests at the banquet would have included executives at the height of their success; but they would have been present as art-lovers and philanthropists. The Martini is the appropriate drink for them. It is tough; it is sensitive. The Martini that Oldenburg serves them repeats in miniature the most common building blocks of their urban habitat: steel, as well as aluminum and Plexiglas, and plastic, which Oldenburg intended to evoke. Oldenburg does not say "American" directly, but his description says it, and his sculpture says it.

The use of steel to represent gin visualizes the metaphor underlying one of gin's nicknames, "liquid steel." Metal for liquid is also the basis of one of the common nicknames of the Martini, "the silver bullet." The other prominent element of the sculpture, the olive, still has its traditional place in the Martini, but from the perspective of the 1990s one sees that Oldenburg's "naturalizing" of this element had in fact anticipated its dislocation from the ethereal unity of the traditional straight-up Martini. A published page from a 1978 notebook shows that he had once thought of the Martini glass as a flashlight and the olive as a flashlight bulb.[3] In that study of the Martini a photograph of the cocktail, apparently from a magazine, is cut in half, at about the midpoint of the stem, and the two sections are separated on the vertical axis. This idea of elongation persisted in *Tilting Neon Cocktail*, but the conceit of the flashlight was abandoned.

Tilting Neon Cocktail captures the two main aspects of the Martini to which this book has been addressed. One is the process of symbolization, an apparently tireless recirculation of meanings, in which Martini drinkers participate. Oldenburg shows, in the relation of *Cocktail* to neon sign, how it works. The other aspect is the drink as phenomenon, as the beautiful symbol behind the neon sign that the sculpture represents. It is the drink fit for millionaires, as Oldenburg well knew, gracing the happy occasions of their and others' lives.

THEORY, METHOD, AND BIBLIOGRAPHY

Food and Drink; Anthropological Approaches; Symbolism

The study of food in sociology and anthropology has attracted some of the most illustrious names in these fields. Theory and method are highly developed. Food also has links to other fields of research—primate behavior and nutrition, to take two obvious examples. Drinking has received less attention, perhaps because it is not a biologically based behavior and seems less important.[1] You have to eat food; you do not have to drink alcoholic drinks. Alcoholic drinks are thus completely in the realm of culture, even if they provide calories and some nutrients, while food presents intriguing interactions of nature and culture. You are what you eat (biology), and you eat what you are (culture). But you drink only what you are (culture); you are not what you drink (no biological correlation). The relation between food and alcoholic drinks is asymmetrical. The latter are liberated from the necessities of nature and thus more fungible in the social domain, more available as a form of social expression.

Why alcoholic drinks should be less interesting than food is unclear to me, but one finds little of the sophistication of the fields named above in the study of nonproblematic, socially harmless drinking. With a few exceptions the literature consists of historical and didactic lore, poems, toasts, songs, defenses of drinking, anecdotes, and miscellaneous, often inaccurate, information. Henry Porter and George Roberts wrote in *Cups and Their Customs* (1863), "As, in this age of progress, most things are raised to the position of a science, we see no reason why Bacchanology (if the term please our readers) should not hold a respectable place, and be entitled to its due *mead* of praise."[2] Despite their hopes, the term "Bacchanology" was accepted neither by lexicographers nor by laymen, and bacchanological works have usually been helter-skelter, not scientific.[3]

For every page of this bacchanological literature worth reading, there are five hundred or a thousand serious pages on alcoholism, temperance movements, and Prohibition. Drinking, especially drinking in America, is, in the historian's perspective, the story of the young "alcoholic republic,"[4] the ensuing temperance movements, the Eighteenth and Twenty-first Amendments, patterns of alcohol consumption, and "neotemperance." Researchers in the social sciences and medicine for their part have almost always treated drinking in its pathological aspects.

Anthropologists were long aware that their approach to drinking was different from that of the historians, social scientists, and medical researchers, even if, as one of them said, "no one had gone into the field with the intention of focusing attention on the subject."[5] In particular, anthropologists treated drinking not as a problem but as a positive force in society. In 1987 Mary Douglas edited a collection of articles by various hands—among them the article just quoted—with the significant title *Constructive Drinking: Perspectives on Drink from Anthropology*. The main division in the articles is indicated by the headings "Drinks Construct the World As It Is" and "Drinks Construct an Ideal World." A third section contains three articles on the role of alcohol in economy. Most of the articles in this collection contain ethnographic data that could be brought into relation with Martini-drinking in the United States, but there is a fundamental difference in approach between these anthropologists and me, as the following titles indicate:

"Longshore Drinking, Economic Security, and Union Politics in Newfoundland"
"*Sekt* versus *Schnapps* in an Austrian Village"
"Varieties of Palm Wine among the Lele of the Ksai"
"*Vin Santo* and Wine in a Tuscan Farmhouse"
"Competitive Beer Drinking among the Mambila"

The authors of these articles were analyzing drinks and or drinking in much smaller groups than the one in which I chose to study the Martini. The worlds to which Mary Douglas refers are relatively small ones and can be described more precisely and exhaustively than I have been able to do in treating the Martini on a vast scale as the national American drink that I believe it is. The Martini could, of course, be studied in some limited group within the United States. I shall return to the problem of the choice of the population and the method of research.

I would describe many of the individual drinks discussed by Douglas's contributors as symbolic, a word that she avoids in her introduction, perhaps because anthropologists tend to look for symbolism in myth, in religious ritual, and in other important ceremonies. She might say that it is not the drink that is important but its use, its social function; that the social function, and thus the social meaning for the observer, lies in the drinking, not in the drink. My emphasis is on the drink, which can carry much symbolic weight in the absence of any ritual, though, as it happens, it sometimes entails a ritual.

In my sense of the Martini as a symbol, I part company not only with the field anthropology of the Douglas collection but also with the structural anthropology and the semiotics that inspired and guided my research when I started in 1978. Roland Barthes's "Wine and Milk" (1972) and other essays in his *Mythologies* were my mental starting-point.[6] I tried to think of drinks as a system of signs and thus as a medium of communication. From Barthes and even more inevitably, considering the period in which I was working, from Claude Lévi-Strauss (*The Raw and the Cooked*, 1970), both of whom got it from Ferdinand de Saussure, I took the idea of the differential basis of the system. I believe that one will have seen this quest for differential criteria at work throughout this book.

But I did not, I now see more clearly, end up in the same place as Barthes and Lévi-Strauss. True to the linguistic basis of their method, they looked for and found systems. The individual items that constituted the system had to have a known value. What was unknown, until the semiotician or structuralist came along, was the system and its cryptic functioning in the mentality of the people using it. For me, the Martini, which I initially thought of as a sign, proved to have much greater complexity than any single item in the works that I was using as models. Further, what seemed to be unknown was the complex of meanings of this one item, whereas the natives, so to speak, seemed to have a good grasp of the system—let's say, the drink code—as a whole. So I would now call the Martini a symbol, having in mind its complexity and ambiguity. Despite what I said about the anthropologists' interest in the loftier symbols—corresponding to others' interest in symbolism in art and literature—I have still been able to find a useful model in their study of this subject.

First, on the matter of the definition of "symbol," the main idea is given pretty clearly in the etymology of the word. It is almost a transliteration from Greek, in which it means "token"—that is, something that stands for something else. The verbal form of the word in Greek means "to compare." So a symbol is like a metaphor. It has two sides. To put it in terms of perception, "The human mind is functioning symbolically when some components of its experience elicit consciousness, beliefs, emotions, and usages, respecting other components of its experience. The former set of components are the 'symbols', and the latter set constitute the 'meaning' of the symbols."[7] One can distinguish and name many kinds of symbols, ranging from words, to the signs in very fixed codes like nautical flags, to religious icons. There are also Freudian symbols, which express an unconscious, repressed meaning that in some cases is held to be constant and universal. The kind of symbol that I am concerned with is material, not verbal, and belongs to a code that, though not necessarily unsystematic, is less systematic than some of the favorite examples of the semioticians.

For the anthropologists, the foremost property of the symbol is condensation. "Many things and actions are represented in a single formation," Victor Turner said.[8] He was harking back to an earlier formulation by Edward Sapir, who said of the symbol, "It expresses a condensation of energy, its actual significance being out of all proportion to the apparent triviality of meaning suggested by its mere form."[9] Because of its power to condense, the symbol can bring together disparate meanings, which are "interconnected by virtue of their common possession of analogous qualities or by association in fact or thought."[10] The Simple Messages of the Martini are interconnected disparate meanings. Further, the symbol can also embrace contradictory meanings. Turner said of one of the symbols that he studied, "We can see how the same dominant symbol, which in one kind of ritual stands for one kind of social group or for one principle of organization, in another kind of ritual stands for another kind of group or principle, and in its aggregate of meanings stands for unity and continuity of the widest Ndembu society, embracing its contradictions." I would say that exactly the same is true of the Martini as an American symbol, in its various appearances—at the three-Martini lunch, at a bar after work, or at home in the company of family and friends, to name some of them. Furthermore, in its Ambiguities the Martini embraces fundamental contradictions of American life.

The anthropologist goes into the field and studies an alien group. How does he know what its symbols mean? In the first place, he consults the natives. Dan Sperber criticized Turner for naivety, arguing that native exegesis must itself be interpreted symbolically.[11] I am in a different position. I am both the observer and an informant, though not the only informant. If I were to try to interpret my own exegeses, I doubt that I could succeed. Where would the regressive reasoning stop? The best I can do is to say, as I am saying in this essay, what their theoretical and methodological origin is (or what I think it is). As an observer, as distinguished from a participant, I am most remote from anthropological practice. My research was sedentary and bibliothecal. I never did research in the field, though on the occasions when I encountered the Martini in bars or at parties, I paid close attention to the drink and to the circumstances of its consumption.

Clearly the kinds of field research displayed in the Douglas collection could be done in various groups of Martini-drinkers in the United States, and I am certain that the results would be interesting. To me, the most interesting thing would be to compare them with my own conclusions concerning the Martini. A less useful model for what I might have done is provided by Pierre Bourdieu's discussion of food—he says little about drink—in *Distinction: A Social Critique of the Judgement of Taste*.[12] He made elaborate, highly detailed analyses of the expenditures on various kinds of food by various groups—for example, teachers, senior executives, professionals, engineers, workers. He also showed himself, in his narrative, a highly sensitive observer of manners, habits, and, in general, lifestyle. But in such an analysis the Martini would turn up only as one item among others, and all that one would learn—it is predictable—is that it is an upper-status drink. The complexity of its symbolism would not emerge.

But Bourdieu's book brings me back to Sperber's doubts about the native informant. The doubts that either a Sperber or a Bourdieu would have about me would have to do with my nonchalance concerning the ideological value of the Simple Messages and of the positive side of the Ambiguities. For Bourdieu, everything is clear: "The mode of expression characteristic of cultural production always depends on the laws of the market in which it is offered."[13] In this perspective I am of course guilty of false consciousness. My native explanations, which seem to me self-evident, are entangled in ideology, and it is this ideology that remains to be explained. But aside from the fact that nothing compels me to accept Bourdieu's premise—and it is a premise, not a revealed truth—I can say in self-defense that I have found that it is precisely as a symbol that the Martini carries an autocritique of its major ideological thrust.

I feel some sympathy with Bourdieu when he says, in implicit opposition to semiotics and structural anthropology, that

> between conditions of existence and practices or representations there intervenes the structuring activity of the agents, who, far from reacting mechanically to mechanical stimulations, respond to the invitations or threats of a world whose meaning they have helped to produce. However, the principle of this structuring activity is not, as an intellectualist or anti-genetic idealism would have it, a system of universal forms or categories but a system of internalized, embodied schemes, which, having been constituted in the course of collective history, are acquired in the course of individual history and function in their *practical* state, for *practice* (and not for the sake of pure knowledge).[14]

This is admirably hard-nosed, in the good old Marxist style, but I am in even greater sympathy with Sapir's description of the same process: "Individual and society, in a never-ending interplay of symbolic gestures, build up the pyramided structure called civilization. In this structure very few bricks touch the ground."[15]

Sources of Evidence for the Martini; Bibliography

My plan of research was to cast my net as widely as possible. Often, surprising convergences were the result—for example, the Martini and the cigar in a haiku by Auden, in a passage in a novel by Sinclair Lewis, in George Burns's formula for longevity, and elsewhere. Even without the surprises, a consistent picture of the symbol emerged. I divide my evidence into the following areas, on which I shall comment one by one:

(1) my own experience with the Martini; (2) fiction and poetry; (3) folklore (jokes, sayings, superstitions, legends of origin); (4) movies and television; (5) oral history; (6) passing references to the Martini in newspapers and magazines; (7) advertising; (8) cartoons; (9) books and articles on the Martini; (10) bartender's guides and manuals of drink recipes, as well as cookbooks that contain drink recipes.

1. FIELD RESEARCH   I commented on field research above.

2. FICTION AND POETRY   For the sake of exposition, I have often talked about fictional characters as if they were real. But a novel's intersection with reality is of concern to me only when it comes to the Martini. When Jack London writes of Burning Daylight in 1910 that "he had long since learned that Martinis had their strictly appointed times and places," I assume that this knowledge is something that corresponds to the knowledge of London's original audience. It is not knowledge that Daylight acquires in the novel, nor is it, as far as I can see, a "ghost chapter" that the reader is expected to supply.

Fiction is very useful for the analysis of the symbolism of the Martini. It is also useful for the historical dimension of this symbolism. London's statement can be combined with one made by John R. Hale in the *Saturday Evening Post* in 1909 (here I am straying into the sixth kind of evidence in my list). He described a sophisticated theater audience that "could recognize a block away a Bronx, Martini or Manhattan."[16] One can see that in the first decade of the twentieth century the Martini already has a particular social identity.

As for my bibliography of fiction, I had hoped that it would be longer, especially for the early days, in this revised edition than it has proven to be. My hope was inspired by two considerations. First, the period of literary history called American Literary Realism begins by convention in 1870, thus in the same decade in which the Martini was probably invented. Second, the new availability of electronic texts—new, that is, since the first edition of this book—led me to think that word searches for "Martini" in relevant authors would be an effective mode of research. I was disappointed. First, the major realist novelists seem to have eschewed the Martini. It is not to be found in Mark Twain or Edith Wharton or William Dean Howells, as far as I can tell. Second, electronic texts for this period are not as plentiful as I had expected. In particular, periodical literature (i.e., fiction in journals) is not well represented. The big "Making of America" project is storing periodicals photographically, and so the texts cannot be searched by word on the computer.

Though fiction is fiction, I take it as part of the "general text" of American culture, and I have not used any illustration from fiction that is not corroborated by evidence from other sources. So let it not be said, as was said in a review of the first edition, that I have privileged literary sources.

3. FOLKLORE   As a sometime folklorist, I know that folklore (jokes, sayings, superstitions) tends to be repetitive. What goes around comes around, with only superficial innovation. Since the first edition of this book, I have not heard a single new Martini joke, nor have I seen one on the websites where such jokes appear. The main reason for this recurrence of the same is not, however, the dullness of joke-tellers but, I think, the synchronic structure that holds together the symbolic meanings of the Martini. The structure does not change, and therefore the folklore surrounding the Martini does not change, or if it does, it only allows additions to the existing stock. Some new jokes came into existence in response to the dryness fetishism of the 1950s. But this fetishism did not disturb the fundamental symbolic structure; and, paradoxically, the more successful a new joke, the sooner it began to look like one that had always been around. The dryness jokes are still told, long after the development that inspired them. For a collection of Martini jokes, see the anonymous *Playboy* article "Fifteen Awful Martini Jokes and One Great Martini" cited under "Books and Articles" below.

4. MOVIES AND TELEVISION   I did new research on movies for the revised edition; I have added nothing new from television, except a comment on *Melrose Place* in the introduction. Two thoughts about film as a source for the Martini:

First, film usually emphasizes one side or the other of the Martini's ambiguity. Either it is the elegant drink par excellence, especially as the conjugal Martini in the Thin Man movies or as the Martini-of-the-relationship. Or it is the drink of alcoholics. In the history of American film, one finds, roughly speaking, that these emphases are sequential. In the 1930s, in post-Prohibition exuberance, elegance; in the 1940s, alcoholism. This generalization is offered as a hypothesis, not as a conclusion, and I owe most of it to a conversation with Eric Spilker.

Second, film, aimed at a mass audience, has to tread lightly in representing the positive side of the Martini's symbolism. The dilemma for the filmmakers is how to represent the Martini as elegant without representing it as also upper-status and therefore offensive to some large segment of the intended audience. The solution is the double-coding of the Martini-drinker or the Martini. The Thin Man is the best example. He is coded in simultaneously upper- and lower-status terms: upper in clothes, accent, leisure, and luxury; lower in anonymity (no education; somewhat obscure background as West Coast detective), friends (mostly crooks and cops), and especially tastes. Asked to take a case, he at first refuses; he is too busy entertaining his wife, who has to be taken to "dances, prize fights, night clubs, and wrestling bouts" (*Shadow of the Thin Man*, 1941). His leisure can be coded in lower-status terms because it depends on his wife's assets. If he had acquired this amount of wealth on his own and if at the same time he had the mannerisms that he does have in all the Thin Man films, he would be unacceptable. His Martini would be not elegant and chummy but upper-status and powerful. As it is, he just likes to drink, and the Martini is one, not the only one, of his preferences.

A film can also double-code the Martini itself. I have already discussed the opening scene of *M*A*S*H* (1970) in Simple Message 1. Two other scenes illustrate the process of recoding. When Trapper, a much-needed chest surgeon, arrives, he is welcomed into the society of Hawkeye and Duke despite his sullenness. The former asks, "Would you like to share a Martini with me?" He would. Hawkeye apologizes for the lack of olives. But Trapper has brought a jar of olives with him. He is already one of them. He must come from one of those families that include Martini olives among the things that they take with them when they leave the city for their summer home. Like the other surgeons, Trapper went to a good college, was a college athlete, and is fond of golf. How can the rest of us identify with these upper-status persons? Well, it's their adolescent rebelliousness in the face of army discipline that makes them charming and likeable. As for the Martini, however, it must be recoded. In a later scene they are toasting marshmallows and eating them as they drink their Martinis. The Martini wasn't, then, a serious upper-status appurtenance of these young surgeons. For them, it was just a reminder of home, like toasted marshmallows. (I never saw a single episode of the long *M*A*S*H* television series, in which, I know, the Martini continued to play a role.)

Here is a final, rather subtle example of double-coding. In the movie *Hustle* (1975), Lieutenant Phil Gaines (Burt Reynolds) of the L.A.P.D. meets in a bar with the mother (Eileen Brennan) of a girl whose murder he is investigating. In order to rise to the occasion, the humdrum woman, who is about to lay bare her soap-operatic life to Lieutenant Gaines, orders a dry Martini. Suitably impressed, he asks, "Do you always order Martinis?" She replies, "Why not? Aren't they sophisticated enough?" And to show how down-to-earth he is, while at the same time conceding the gambit, he says, "I never know what to do with the olive." So neither of them is really a drinker of the Martini as an upper-status drink, though Lieutenant Gaines gracefully allows the woman's pretension.

The Martini in the film *Swingers* (1996), about which I wrote in the introduction, is something else altogether. It presupposes a generation gap in which the Martini disappeared. The drink was then free to return in an entirely positive sense as an element in a larger retro style.

5. ORAL HISTORY   I wrote in the first edition that "oral history is an important way of studying drinks and drinking, for the simple reason that so much information exists only in this form and is being carried to the grave every day and probably every hour. It would be wonderful to be able to interview a hundred suitable men and women of eighty years or more."[17] Little did I know that I would someday produce a revised edition of this book and that this statement would come back to haunt me. The Grim Reaper has done his work. The generation of Dorothy Wilson (mentioned, in this edition, in "Historical Background of the Ambiguities"), which could have told me much about the Martini in the teens of this century, is gone. There are still some, but not many, who remember the Martini in the twenties. Within the constraints of time imposed and self-imposed for this revised edition, I could not undertake an oral history. But this time I know that my work continues after the publication of the book, and I shall take every opportunity to question suitable persons about the Martini of their youth.

The National Digital Library Program of the Library of Congress may someday provide documents preserving memories that will add to the picture that I have started to put together in this book. As the holdings of specialized libraries and archives and of historical societies come on line in a searchable format, a compensation for lost oral history will become available.

6. NEWSPAPER AND MAGAZINE REFERENCES   The Martini is proverbial. It stands for alcoholic strength, individuality, WASPishness, and so on, corroborating the analysis of the Martini's symbolism that I have offered. As a proverb, it often appears in newspapers and magazines, as well as in everyday speech. The *New York Times* alone seems to contain several references per week to the Martini.

In passing, a couple of examples. "The Martini" is a Hollywood expression for the last shot of the day.[18] But, thanks to its fabled potency, the Martini will perhaps more often stand for a jolt to the system. In an interview, the poet Philip Larkin identified the chromatic scale as the innovation by which Charlie Parker wrecked jazz. Said Larkin: "The chromatic scale is what you use to give the effect of drinking a quinine martini and having an enema simultaneously."[19]

7. ADVERTISING   Advertising has always interrupted the symbolic order, reshaped the symbol, and then reinserted it into the order, of

course without undue disturbance. The process is strikingly clear in the series of Martini glasses designed for the Bombay Sapphire Gin advertisements of the 1990s. So advertisements prove to reveal the process of symbolization. I discussed Hilton McConnico's redesign of the Martini glass in the introduction and have referred to other advertising in the course of the book.

8. CARTOONS Advertising is innovative and avant-garde; cartoons are conservative. The accompanying table provides a list of Martini cartoons in the *New Yorker* supplied me by the staff of that magazine in 1979 and then updated for me by Jill Frisch in 1997. (Martini cartoons appear in other magazines. It would not be easy to compile a bibliography.) I have supplied the total for each year.

If one analyzed these cartoons, one would find that the same images and the same themes come back again and again. By now a genre has been established, and each new cartoon will refer not only to the Martini but also to antecedent Martini cartoons. Reference to the contemporary Martini will be from a strictly conservative point of view. Thus, as I have pointed out, the conjugal Martini persists in cartoons of the 1990s. As for the pattern of frequency, the 1960s has, not unexpectedly, the greatest number of blank years. The balloon in the 1980s probably corresponds to "the return of the Martini" that was a theme of newspaper and magazine articles on the Martini in the decade. It was always linked, perhaps correctly, with the yuppies.

9. BOOKS AND ARTICLES The theme was so insistent that finally, in the May 1989 issue of *Playboy*, Glenn O'Brien published an article called "Every Year There's an Article Called 'The Return of the Martini.'" I found this title in some database or other but did not bother to look it up because the abstract said, "LaToya Jackson's recent nude appearance in *Playboy* is discussed." So I do not know what the relation of the title to the article is, but the title by itself had a certain truth. I was much aware of the "return" theme, because reporters often called me about the Martini in the 1980s. I have not, however, attempted to update the bibliography of newspapers and magazines that I published in the first edition, with the exception of Max Rudin's article and a couple of others that seemed worthwhile. The electronic databases make it easy enough to find these things, although the ones in in-flight magazines and trade publications may still be ephemeral.

Among the countless articles on the Martini are:

Anon. "Fifteen Awful Martini Jokes and One Great Martini." *Playboy*, Mar. 1974, 95, 167.

MARTINI CARTOONS IN THE *NEW YORKER*, 1949–1997

Year	Total	
1949	1	18 June, p. 18
1950	0	
1951	0	
1952	1	14 June, p. 37
1953	0	
1954	1	10 July, p. 32
1955	0	
1956	4	25 Feb., p. 31; 17 Mar., p. 47; 24 Nov., p. 57; 1 Dec., p. 45
1957	1	9 Mar., p. 25
1958	0	
1959	1	24 Jan., p. 32
1960	1	12 Nov., p. 103
1961	0	
1962	0	
1963	2	23 Feb., p. 39; 31 Aug., p. 29
1964	1	21 Nov., p. 236
1965	0	
1966	1	4 June, p. 39
1967	3	7 Jan., p. 18; 4 Feb., p. 35; 5 Aug., pp. 28–29
1968	0	
1969	3	17 May, p. 33; 31 May, p. 85; 8 Nov., p. 64
1970	0	
1971	4	3 Apr., p. 44; 22 May, p. 37; 2 Oct., p. 98; 27 Nov., p. 89
1972	3	11 Mar., p. 38; 3 June, p. 81; 21 Oct., p. 38
1973	1	22 Oct., p. 142
1974	1	11 Feb., p. 102
1975	1	10 Mar., p. 32
1976	2	1 Mar., p. 55; 29 Nov., p. 37
1977	2	13 June, p. 40; 26 Dec., p. 28
1978	4	6 Feb., p. 31; 17 July, p. 31; 18 Sept., p. 44; 23 Oct., p. 46
1979	3	8 Jan., p. 53; 5 Mar., p. 40; 24 Dec., p. 31
1980	1	6 Oct., p. 48
1981	8	2 Mar., p. 49; 16 Mar., p. 38; 15 June, p. 56; 13 July, p. 85; 17 Aug., p. 31; 31 Aug., p. 35; 28 Sept., p. 121; 12 Oct., p. 53
1982	5	22 Mar., p. 61; 14 June, p. 108; 24 May, p. 82; 20 Sept., p. 51; 1 Nov., p. 34
1983	5	3 Jan, p. 57; 14 Feb., p. 49; 28 Feb., p. 82; 19 Sept., p. 140; 26 Sept., p. 52
1984	4	23 Jan., p. 86; 12 Mar., p. 125; 29 Oct., p. 38; 5 Nov., p. 61
1985	3	11 Mar., p. 45; 15 Apr., p. 51; 30 Dec., p. 53
1986	3	3 Feb., p. 22; 24 Mar., p. 41; 15 Dec., p. 34
1987	2	25 May, p. 113; 28 Sept., p. 63
1988	3	4 Jan., p. 23; 11 Apr., p. 109; 12 Dec., p. 148
1989	2	31 July, p. 75; 16 Oct., p. 54
1990	1	30 Dec., p. 36
1991	2	7 Jan., p. 26; 24 June, p. 35
1992	2	30 Mar., p. 38; 28 Sept., p. 41
1993	0	
1994	3	19 Sept., p. 64; 3 Oct., p. 78; 21 Nov., p. 95
1995	0	
1996	3	5 Aug., p. 49; 30 Sept., p. 73; 25 Nov., p. 56
1997	4	6 Jan., p. 61; 19 May, p. 76; 23 and 30 June, p. 146; 13 Oct., p. 77

Anon. "The Martini Era." *Liquor Store,* Jan. 1968, 15–22.

Anon. "The Special Role of the Martini." *Liquor Store,* Feb. 1967, 25–26.

DeVoto, Bernard. "For the Wayward and Beguiled." In "The Easy Chair," a regular column. *Harper's,* Dec. 1949, 68–71. Reprinted, with revisions, in *The Hour* (Boston: Houghton Mifflin, 1951).

Fisher, M. F. K. "To the Gibson and Beyond." *Atlantic,* Jan. 1949, 93–94.

————. "Martini-Zheen Anyone?" *Gourmet,* Jan. 1957, 14.

Frail, F. S. "In Search of the Perfect Martini." *Savor* (magazine supplement of the *Boston Phoenix*), 29 May 1979, 6.

Gonzales, Donald J. "Crisis at the Cocktail Hour." *Saturday Review,* 15 Nov. 1975, 46–48.

Graham, J. A. Maxtone. "The Martini." *Gourmet,* Nov. 1968, 27.

Malamud, Daniel, and Mary H. Murphy. "Martini Toothpick Warning." Letter to the editor. *New England Journal of Medicine* 315 (16 Oct. 1986): 1031–32. Reprinted in B. H. Kean, *M.D.: One Doctor's Adventures among the Famous and Infamous from the Jungles of Panama to a Park Avenue Practice* (New York: Ballantine Books, 1990), 96–97, with the erroneous information that the letter is "from an article." It is only a letter to the editor.

Morgan, Jefferson. "Whatever Happened to the Martini?" *Bon Appetit,* Oct. 1978, 73–74.

Rudin, Max. "'There Is Something about a Martini.'" *American Heritage* 48, no. 4 (July–Aug. 1997): 32–51.

Schwartz, Allen. "The Mythology and Mixology of the Martini." *The Server,* Jan.–Feb. 1966, 23–33.

Tamony, Peter. "Martini Cocktail." *Western Folklore* 26, no. 2 (1967): 124–27.

Villas, James. "The Social Status of the Martini." *Esquire,* Apr. 1973, 111–12.

I have quoted repeatedly from Fisher and DeVoto—from the latter in particular because his article is a compendium of typical attitudes. Of the others, Graham, Rudin, and Schwartz contain the most information.

As for books, William Grimes's *Straight Up or On the Rocks: A Cultural History of American Drink* (New York: Simon and Schuster, 1993) contains a chapter on the Martini. Books entirely on the Martini are:

Conrad, Barnaby, III. *The Martini: An Illustrated History of an American Classic.* San Francisco: Chronicle Books, 1995.

Doxat, John. *Stirred—Not Shaken: The Dry Martini.* London: Hutchinson Benham, 1976.

Herzbrun, Robert. *The Perfect Martini Book.* New York and London: Harcourt Brace Jovanovich, 1979.

Miller, Anistatia R., and Jared M. Brown. *Shaken Not Stirred: A Celebration of the Martini.* New York: HarperPerennial, 1997.

10. BARTENDER'S GUIDES AND THE LIKE   The earliest reference to the Martini occurs in a bartender's manual of 1884; the earliest reference in literature is in a short story in 1896.[20] For a decade or so of its history, then, the Martini is known only from bartender's manuals. These provide mainly recipes but sometimes also contain other information. The relation between these two sources, the how-to books and literature, will change as new references to the Martini in the latter source come to light. (Cf. what I said under "Fiction and Poetry" above.) For now, the former source is most important for the 1880s and 1890s.

Several manuals from the 1880s have gone missing. They were missing at the time of my research for the first edition, and they are still missing. I have spent a great deal of my time and others' time searching for them. They are marked with an asterisk in the list below, and unless otherwise noted, no living person known to me has seen them. An asterisk also marks a few books that someone else has seen and told me about; I have so indicated. (I corresponded in 1981 with the J. F. Hansman to whom I refer. He was working on a history of the cocktail. I was unsuccessful in my attempt to reestablish contact with him.) I have heard again and again from specialist book dealers that early American bartender's manuals have become a fad with European, especially German and Swiss, collectors. Nach Waxman of Kitchen Arts and Letters in New York put me in touch with Hans Surber in Zurich, who in turn gave me the addresses of several dealers in his own country and in Germany. I received no reply to my letters to these persons.

Cookbooks and books of household management that contain drink recipes are another useful source for the early history of the Martini. A couple of them are cited below. My bibliography is likely to be quite incomplete in this respect.

I have arranged the following bibliography by date. All authors and titles are also listed in the Index.

1862. Thomas, Jerry. *How to Mix Drinks, or The Bon Vivant's Companion.* New York. Cf. 1876 and 1887.

1866. Monzert, L. *The Independent Liquorist.* New York.

1869.* Anon. *The Steward and Bartender's Manual.* New York. Seen by J. F. Hansman.

1869. Haney, Jesse. *Steward and Barkeeper's Manual.* New York.

1871.* Anon. *Bartender's Ready Reference.* Place of publication unknown. Seen by J. F. Hansman.

1876. Thomas, Jerry. *How to Mix Drinks, or The Bon Vivant's Companion.* New York. Cf. 1862 and 1887.

1880. Engel, Leo. *American and Other Drinks.* London.

1882.* Johnson, Harry. *New and Improved Illustrated Bartender's Manual, or How to Mix Drinks of the Present Style.* New York. Seen by J. F. Hansman.

1883. McDonough, P. *McDonough's Bar-keeper's Guide.* Rochester, N.Y.

1884. Barnes, Albert. *The Complete Bartender.* Philadelphia.

1884. Byron, O. H. *The Modern Bartender's Guide.* New York.

1884. Gibson, J. W. *Scientific Barkeeping.* Buffalo.

1884. Naber, Alf and Brune. *Catalogue and Bartender's Guide.* San Francisco.

1884.* Winter, G. *How to Mix Drinks.* New York.

1886.* Laird, W. H. *American Bartender.* St. John's, New Brunswick.

1887. Thomas, Jerry. *How to Mix Drinks, or The Bon Vivant's Companion.* New York. Cf. 1862 and 1876.

1888.* Concklin, J. *The Bartender.* New York.

1888. Johnson, Harry. *New and Improved Illustrated Bartender's Manual, or How to Mix Drinks of the Present Style.* New York.

1889.* Casey, E. M. *The Mixologist and Compounder.* San Francisco.

1891. Boothby, William T. *Cocktail Boothby's American Bartender.* San Francisco.

1891.* Newman, Lewis P. *Newman's Book on Scientific Barkeeping.* Fayetteville, N.C.

1891.* Peck, J. E. *Fancy Drinks and How to Mix Them.* New York.

1891. Wehman, H. J. *Wehman's Bartender's Guide.* New York.

1892. The Only William (A. William Schmidt). *The Flowing Bowl: When and What to Drink.* New York.

1893. Ranhofer, Charles. *The Epicurean.* Chicago. The copy I saw was published in 1920, but it reprinted a letter by Mr. Delmonico dated 1893, recommending the book (a cookbook, with a section on drinks).

1895. Green, H. W. *Mixed Drinks.* Indianapolis, Ind.

1895. Kappeler, George J. *Modern American Drinks.* Akron, Ohio.

1895. Lawlor, C. F. *The Mixologist.* Cincinnati.

1896. Lamore, H. *The Bartender.* New York.

1896. Stiles, H. W. *The Chapin and Gore Manual.* Chicago.

1896. Stuart, Thomas. *Stuart's Fancy Drinks.* Reprint, New York: Excelsior Publishing House, 1904.

1898. Anon. *Cocktails: How to Make Them.* Providence, R.I.

Theory, Method, and Bibliography

1898. Haywood, J. L. *Mixology*. Wilmington, Del.

1899.* Spencer, Edward. *The Flowing Bowl: A Treatise on Drinks of All Kinds and of All Periods, etc.* London and New York. Seen by Leah Edmunds.

1900. [Knowles, Frederic Lawrence.] *The Cocktail Book: A Sideboard Manual for Gentlemen.* Boston: L. C. Page.

1902* or earlier. Didier, Jack. Title is either *Reminder* or *Didier's Reminder.* Binghamton, N.Y.

1903. Daly, Tim. *Daly's Bartender's Encyclopedia.* Worcester, Mass.

1904. Lowe, Paul E. *Drinks As They Are Mixed.* Chicago: Frederick J. Drake.

1906. Beeton, Isabella. *Mrs. Beeton's Book of Household Management.* London.

1906.* Muckensturm, L. J. *Louis' Mixed Drinks.* Boston.

In the quest for the missing titles I was sometimes asked, "Have you looked in Noling?" I used A. W. Noling, *Beverage Literature: A Bibliography* (Metuchen, N.J.: Scarecrow, 1971), in my research for the first edition, and I cited him in that edition. It should be understood that Noling is unreliable in two respects. First, he was not thorough enough. (I may be unreliable for the same reason.) For Stuart (1896) and for Spencer (1899), for example, Noling cites only later editions. Often one suspects that he is simply copying out the first reference that came to hand—for example, from the National Union Catalogue or some other library catalogue. Second, through no fault of his own, books that he had probably seen are no longer where he saw them. For example, some of those marked with an asterisk in my list were once in the Hurty-Peck Beverage Library—which Noling visited, I believe, when it was in Indianapolis—but cannot be found in the library's new location at the University of California at Davis. In sum, Noling is a valuable source, but nothing is going to be settled by an appeal to him.

The Future of Martini Research

Much remains to be done, above all on the history of the Martini glass (see the appendix). All of the sources I have listed deserve separate studies—jokes, cartoons, advertising, and so forth. A bibliography of early cookbooks and books of household management is needed. More work on the bibliography of early bartender's manuals just presented is needed. In that connection one would want a good list of the special collections of drink-related books in the United States and abroad. No such list exists at present. Much research in the periodical literature and fiction of the period called American Literary Realism is needed.

APPENDIX: THE MARTINI GLASS

This appendix often refers to the drawings in Figure 11. Not all of the sources for these drawings indicated the scale. It was therefore impossible to represent the relative sizes, and a uniform scale was applied. In the following notes on the sources, I include whatever information on size was available.

1. From catalogue of Cascade Glass Works (Pittsburgh). "Cocktail." Ca. 1870. Height: approx. 5 inches.
2. From catalogue of Cascade Glass Works (Pittsburgh). "Cocktail." Ca. 1870. Height: approx. 5 inches.
3. From catalogue of O'Hara Glass Company (Pittsburgh). "Cocktail flared." Ca. 1885. Height: approx. 5 inches.
4. From catalogue of O'Hara Glass Company (Pittsburgh). "Cocktail saucer." Ca. 1885. Height: approx. 5 inches.
5. From a postcard by Samuel Schmucker, published by Detroit Publishing Company. "Martini." 1907. It is one of a set of six, each one representing a different glass. The others are Manhattan, Champagne, Sherry, Claret, and Crème de Menthe.
6. Fredrick Carder catalogue drawing (Steuben).[1] 7587. "Martini." Height 5½ inches. Late 1920s–early 1930s.
7. Fredrick Carder catalogue drawing (Steuben).[2] 7630. "Martini." Diameter of bowl: 3⅛ inches. Diameter of base: 2½ inches. Late 1920s–early 1930s.
8. Fredrick Carder catalogue drawing (Steuben).[3] 7284. Glass not named. Late 1920s.

As the introduction to this book showed, the Martini glass was the vehicle of the Martini's return in the 1990s, and so firmly established was the glass as a cultural icon that it could be redesigned as a nonfunctional art object. Claes Oldenburg had anticipated the trend with his Pop Art sculpture *Tilting Neon Cocktail* (1983). The glass poses intriguing historical and interpretive questions. When was the stemmed glass with conical bowl first manufactured in the United States? When did it become associated with the Martini? (The two developments were separate.) Why did it become associated with the Martini? None of these questions can at present be answered satisfactorily, and this appendix can do little more than define the problems.

As for the first question, research begins in the nineteenth century. "Historical Background of the Ambiguities" gives an indication of the origin of the cocktail and of the Martini. One would like to coordinate the

« FIGURE II »
Glasses ca. 1870–early 1930s
Sketched by Leah Edmunds
from material in the Leonard S. and Juliette K. Rakow Library
of the Corning Museum of Glass

history of the drinks with the history of glassware. Unfortunately, the latter history has not been written, and I doubt that there exists even so much as a typology of nineteenth-century American drinking-glass forms. One is thrown back on catalogues of glass manufacturers and other, miscellaneous sources such as illustrations in bartender's manuals, in magazines, and in books on household management. (My research in these latter areas was exiguous. At the time I was looking through the bartender's manuals cited in "Theory, Method, and Bibliography," which had been borrowed from libraries around the country, I was not thinking about the history of the Martini glass. Somehow in 1977 or 1978 I captured the illustration in Harry Johnson's manual [Figure 6]. Now I wonder if there were others.)

From the catalogues I have seen, which include seven others besides those listed above, I think that a standard morphology begins to develop in the 1870s. The only earlier catalogue I have seen is that of the New England Glass Company (ca. 1869).[4] (So the statement with which this paragraph begins may be an inductive leap.) This catalogue contains no cocktail glass but cordial, wine, and champagne glasses, and goblets in two shapes, "round bowl" and "flanged," which at first glance are indistinguishable, so subtle is the flange. But these two shapes then reappear in glasses designated as "cocktail" in the 1870s. Compare sketches 1 and 2 in Figure 11, which appear only a year or so after the goblets just mentioned. These shapes, with slight variations, remain constant, as sketches 3 and 4, from 1885, show. The catalogue (O'Hara Glass Company, Pittsburgh) in which 3 and 4 appear provides some terms: "Cocktail flared" and "Cocktail saucer." Other catalogues from the 1870s and 1880s show these same two shapes, which are clearly the preponderant ones.[5]

The flat-bottomed bowl, of the kind seen in Harry Johnson's manual (Figure 6) is much rarer. I take Johnson's illustration, by the way, as an illustration of the Martini (or "Martine") and not of a Martini glass, but it does show a glass that was considered appropriate for the Martini in 1888.

As for sketch 5, which is the earliest glass (1907) that I have found that is designated "Martini," it is anomalous. Its open, slightly curved bowl has no obvious predecessor. Max Rudin suggested to me that it is a development of the champagne coupe, but no nineteenth-century coupe that I have seen looks like a model for it, and I would add that the cone-shaped bowl that now means Martini glass cannot be regarded as an evolution of the champagne coupe. The artist who drew the Martini glass and five others for the set of postcards was of course aiming at maximum differentiation; his graphic skill was not great, in my opinion; and a desire to represent faithfully the glassware of his time cannot be assumed.[6]

I would go further and affirm that any evolutionary view of the history of the Martini glass will be incorrect. The cone-shaped bowl had been in existence for a long time and was a perennial possibility. Consider the Venetian glass (ca. 1575–1625) in Figure 12. Designers could and did reintroduce the v-shaped profile in the midst of other, morphologically unrelated lines. Fredrick Carder did so in a line of eight glasses for Steuben in the 1910s, none of them designated a cocktail or Martini glass.[7] The Cambridge Glass Company did the same thing in the period 1928–38—a set of eleven different glasses, including a finger bowl, in the v-shaped profile. It includes a 3½ oz. cocktail glass. The 6 oz. sherbet glass in this line would also today be perceived as a Martini glass. Dorothy Carpenter Thorpe designed a similar series in the 1930s.[8] At some point the designers and manufacturers are, of course, imitating each other. But the origin of the cone-shaped bowl in the history of American glassware has to be understood as a marketing strategy, not as an evolution of style. The earliest example I have encountered is Carder's line—to repeat, it did not include a Martini glass—but it would not be surprising if earlier American examples turned up.

The second question that I posed was, When did the cone-shaped bowl become associated with the Martini? Not soon, is the best answer

« FIGURE 12 »
Glass from Murano, Italy, ca. 1575–1625
The Newark Museum/Art Resource, New York

I can give. Sketches 6 and 7 in Figure 11, both from the late 1920s–early 1930s, are of glasses that Carder labeled "Martini." The bowl is not yet the cone-shaped one. Their antecedents in the nineteenth-century saucer and flared shapes are obvious. In Carder's mind, and no doubt in the mind of his intended market, these shapes are appropriate for the Martini. The design of Carder's third Martini glass (sketch 8)—the applied olive identifies it clearly enough—is the one that was to become definitive for the Martini, but even by the end of the 1930s it had not yet become de rigueur. Magazine advertisements and also films of that decade show the Martini being drunk from a wide variety of glasses.[9] The 1940s, as Ulysses Dietz has suggested to me, is the decade in which it finally happens.

The Martini glass, as we can now call it, becomes a basic American symbol—not perhaps as universal as the cowboy, blue jeans, or Coca-Cola, but almost. As for Coca-Cola, a similar linking of a drink and a vessel occurred. The Coke bottle, to which the drink's worldwide success is mainly owed, was designed in 1916, thirty years after the drink was invented. Once invented, however, the drink became inseparable from the image, while the image acquired a life of its own, along with the graphics of the Coca-Cola logo.[10] So far the story is like the story of the Martini and the Martini glass: the drink becomes inseparable from its container, and the latter becomes an image in its own right. But the design of the Coke bottle was ultimately determined by considerations of manufacturing, and the designers were not influenced by the momentous changes in the history of style that were happening all around them. (Just visualize a Coke bottle.) The Martini glass, even if it was, as I have said, an age-old design possibility, must have caught on because it was perceived as new and stylish. The Art Deco features of the cocktail set in Figure 8 (1929) establish a context of reception for the cone-shaped bowl. Whatever the shape meant to, say, the designer of the Venetian glass in Figure 12, in the late 1920s it meant au courant. One can broaden the context to include Cubist painting, De Stijl, and the Bauhaus. The eye was ready for the geometric shape of the Martini glass.

Why was the Martini cocktail linked to this glass (or vice versa)? Probably because the cocktail too was perceived as being au courant, even though it had been around for forty or fifty years. The 1920s bring in a new class of drinkers, including women, and new styles of drinking—for example, the cocktail party. Prohibition makes gin the favorite distilled spirit. Gin makes the Martini a favorite cocktail (see "Historical Background of the Ambiguities"). In this social context, then, the Martini is perceived as new and is at home in the new (again, as perceived) glass. It catches on, and then stays on. As Max Rudin said, "As formally harmonious with the zigzags of Art Deco, as with the hourglass shapes of the fifties 'New Look', the martini glass is one of the few designs to make a seamless transition from moderne to modern."[11]

This historical sketch does not, I think, contradict Simple Message 7 (the Martini belongs to the past, not to the present). If new meant radically new or revolutionary or even avant-garde, I do not see how, at the end of the 1940s, Cold Warriors, business types, and cultural troglodytes could be merrily drinking Martinis from the geometric Martini glass, as we know that they were. What happened, as often happens in the United States, was that the new was instantly adapted to life, became routine, and was therefore as good as old. The Martini cocktail, as distinguished from the glass, was new, after all, only if one chose to regard it as such, and some significant percentage of Martini drinkers in, say, 1935 would have been drinking Martinis in 1905 or earlier. For them, the Martini was not new. As for the glass, the history of modernist architecture in the United States in the corresponding period (1930–50) shows the same rapid acceptance that renders the new unobtrusive, familiar, and soon normal. The modernist corporate headquarters takes its place in the visual imagery of business along with the older business suit, which belongs to a history of style going back to the nineteenth century.

Another characteristic of the Martini glass that might have helped to secure its acceptance is its elegant restriction of functionality. With the flat sides of its bowl and its slender, sometimes elongated stem (see sketch 8), it is a glass from which a drink is easily spilled. Thus the fascination with which Evelyn Waugh observed the Martini glasses gently rocking on the table in a club car: "The little circle of gin and vermouth in the glasses lengthened to oval, contracted again, with the sway of the carriage, touched the lip, lapped back again, never spilt" (see Ambiguity 2 for the rest of the passage). The drink has to be sipped. The drinker has to be civilized.[12]

Finally, just as the Martini is the overdetermined alcoholic drink, gathering to itself all the associations, good and bad, of distilled spirits and of drinking, so the glass acquired a sexual association that all glasses and cups have, though they have it less specifically and less (dare I say it?) pointedly. Max Rudin said that the Martini glass was harmonious with "the hourglass shapes of the fifties." He was probably thinking of the profile of the glass, and Barnaby Conrad was thinking of its centerline when he said, "It is as poised as a ballerina on point and its contents must be imbibed with care."[13] In both cases these civilized writers were responding to the glass in its two-dimensional look. As a three-dimensional thing, however, the bowl or cup of the glass is an image of the female breast. The riddle cited earlier in this book asks why a Martini is like a woman's breasts (Ambiguity 1). A deeper answer can now be offered. The association of drinking vessel and breast goes back to antiquity, as Adrienne Mayor shows in her article on the subject.[14] The best-known example in modern times is the four Sèvres porcelain cups made in a mold taken from Marie Antoinette's breast. In fact the very first Martini glass that is identified as such, on the postcard already discussed, had a woman sitting in it (she was not included in sketch 5). The theme continues up to the present. Mel Ramos's oil painting *Martini Miss,* a naked woman in a Martini glass, is a striking example.[15] Mayor has argued that the woman in such representations is a synecdoche for the breast.[16]

NOTES

Introduction

1. Bernard DeVoto, *The Hour* (Boston: Riverside, 1951), 22; Alistair Cooke, *Six Men* (New York: Alfred A. Knopf, 1977), 94.

2. Charles E. Bohlen, *Witness to History: 1929–1969* (New York: W. W. Norton, 1973), 43.

3. John Doxat, *Stirred—Not Shaken: The Dry Martini* (London: Hutchinson Benham, 1976), 134. Doxat's source was Ronnie Stammers, bartender on the *Queen Elizabeth II*.

4. Georges Simenon, *Intimate Memoirs*, trans. H. J. Salemson (San Diego: Harcourt Brace Jovanovich, 1984), 388, on the year 1954: on occasion he drinks "a very chilled dry Martini, in which the gin is now often replaced by vodka." There is a not very enlightening article on Simenon's drinking: Donald W. Goodwin, "The Muse and the Martini," *Journal of the American Medical Association* 224 (2 Apr. 1973): 35–38. For Simenon's analysis of his drinking, see his *When I Was Old*, trans. Helen Eustis (New York: Harcourt Brace Jovanovich, 1971), 197ff.

In Tennessee Williams's *Sweet Bird of Youth* (first performed 10 Mar. 1959), act 2, scene 2, in St. Cloud, a town on the Gulf Coast, in a hotel bar, Chance, reacting to his first sip of a Martini, tells the bartender, "Man, don't you know . . . phew . . . nobody drinks gin martinis with olives. Everybody drinks vodka martinis with lemon twist nowadays, except the squares in St. Cloud."

5. William Grimes, *Straight Up or On the Rocks: A Cultural History of American Drink* (New York: Simon and Schuster, 1993); Barnaby Conrad III, *The Martini: An Illustrated History of an American Classic* (San Francisco: Chronicle Books, 1995); Max Rudin, "'There Is Something about a Martini,'" *American Heritage* 48, no. 4 (July–Aug. 1997): 32–51.

6. The latter is manufactured by Neon Source, Inc., and distributed by the Sharper Image.

7. Designed by Anistatia R. Miller and Jared M. Brown. For further information, see their website, http://www.martinis.com/key/.

8. The glass is 6¾ inches tall, and the diameter of the bowl is 4¼ inches. The cost of two glasses is $380.

9. *New York Times*, 4 Dec. 1996, C6.

10. The expression was coined by Byron Werner of Los Angeles "to describe a genre of Eisenhower-Kennedy era instrumental pop. Werner summed up the style in a 1990 interview in the desktop publication *Audio Carpaetorium*: 'use of a theremin, discordant harmonies, exaggerated stereo effects, zippy, optimistic melodies'. The phrase entered the collector's lexicon, and was adapted [*sic*] in 1993 by the British band Stereolab as an album title." Irwin Chisud, liner notes in the CD ¡*Viva, Esquivel!* (1994).

11. Judy Bachrach, "'Tinis, 'Tails, and Tippling," *Allure*, Apr. 1996, 202.

12. Though early recipes sometimes call for an olive, it was not until sometime in the 1930s or later that it came to be one of the routine garnishes, the other being the zest of lemon that is first twisted over the surface of the drink. For the olive as a lower-status garnish, see Frank Shay, "The Best Cocktails of

1934," *Esquire*, Dec. 1934, 40: "In New York, the Martini seems to be the Citizen's choice at the best bars, and by best bars I mean not only those places whose patrons realize that a Martini at a quarter or thirty cents is a good buy, but those places that have sent the olive back, without comment, to wherever it is that olives belong." Bernard DeVoto, writing in the late forties, was adamantly opposed to the olive. See his "For the Wayward and Beguiled" ("The Easy Chair"), *Harper's Magazine*, Dec. 1949, 68–71.

13. Anistatia R. Miller and Jared M. Brown, *Shaken Not Stirred: A Celebration of the Martini* (New York: HarperPerennial, 1997).

14. *New York Times*, 4 Dec. 1996, C1.

15. *Entertainment Weekly*, 12 Sept. 1997, 52. Note that the exchange of the verbs "swill" and "sip" between their expected places—the first goes with beer, the second with Martinis—constitutes the rhetorical figure called hypallage.

16. Michael Jaross, e-mail to Lowell Edmunds, 22 June 1997. Jaross's work can be seen in major galleries throughout the United States and has appeared in *American Craft Magazine*, Feb.–Mar. 1995, and in *New Glass Review* 14 (1993) and 16 (1995).

17. *New Yorker*, 19 May 1997, 76. The cartoon is by Smaller.

18. Jerry Della Femina, "The Hey-Day of the Three-Martini Lunch," *New York Times Magazine*, 28 Oct. 1989, 22.

19. Linda Hutcheon, *A Poetics of Postmodernism* (New York: Routledge, 1988), 26, 126.

20. Donald G. Smith, "To the Young, Vermouth Is a State," *Wall Street Journal*, 9 Dec. 1985, sec. 1, p. 24.

MESSAGE ONE

Epigraph: George Watson, "I Was Kingsley Amis," *Hudson Review* 49 (1997): 610–18, at 613.

1. Dean Acheson, "Robert Shuman," in *Sketches from Life of Men I Have Known* (New York: Harper and Brothers, 1961), 41.

2. Christopher Fildes, "Martini Time—It's My Moment of Madness and Lamont's Unhappy Hour," *Spectator*, 29 Aug. 1991, 22.

3. Jim Gordon, "The Ten-Martini Lunch," *Wine Spectator*, Jan. 1994. "Eleven to one" is the ratio of gin to vermouth. I read the story in the magazine's electronic archives and was unable to obtain the page number. I have also heard the story from Apple himself, in a telephone conversation, 10 Sept. 1997.

4. *Gourmet*, Jan. 1957, 15.

5. *Boston Sunday Globe*, 25 June 1978, 29.

6. Pearl S. Buck, *Mandala* (New York: John Day, 1970), 194–95.

7. W. Somerset Maugham, "The Fall of Edward Barnard," in *The Trembling of a Leaf* (New York: G. H. Doran, 1921), 96–97.

8. Directed by Robert Altman; screenplay by Ring Lardner Jr. The title is an acronym for Mobile Army Surgical Hospital. The television series went on from 17 Sept. 1972 to 19 Sept. 1983.

MESSAGE TWO

Epigraph: Bernard DeVoto, *The Hour* (Boston: Houghton Mifflin, 1951), 78.

1. Patsy McDonough, *McDonough's Bar-keeper's Guide* (Rochester, N.Y., 1883), 5.

2. Barnaby Conrad III, *The Martini: An Illustrated History of an American Classic* (San Francisco: Chronicle Books, 1995), 55–56. The attribution to Butterworth of course depends on the reliability of Wilder's recollection.

3. This attribution was as far as I had gotten at the time of the first edition of this book. The story is still interesting. Mr. Howard M. Teichmann, in the course of research for his biography of George S. Kaufman, discovered that the source was not Woollcott but Robert Benchley, and the biography contains a statement to this effect. Russell Baker somehow acquired this piece of information, although I do not know if Teichmann was his source, and in "Babble, Babble, Glub-Glub," his *New York Times* column for 13 Dec. 1977, he wrote about Irvin Candora, who was not "into" anything, but "sometimes . . . slipped out of a heavy rain and into a dry martini, out of respect for Robert Benchley." Baker seems to assume that everyone knows the saying and that it came from Robert Benchley. The second of these assumptions is likely to be unfounded. In any case, Mr. Teichmann wrote to me that he later learned from Nathaniel Benchley, the son of Robert (and the father of the author of *Jaws*), that the saying was the brainchild of Benchley's press agent, who passed it on to a columnist as Benchley's own.

4. The Martini-man will stop at nothing. During a blackout in 1966, Mr. Lester A. Rodin, deprived of ice from his refrigerator, suspended a cupful of Martini in a wide-necked thermos flask of liquid nitrogen and inserted a stick into the drink as it froze. He thus became the inventor of the "Martini-sicle." Allen Schwartz, "The Mythology and Mixology of the Martini," *The Server*, Jan.–Feb. 1966, 26–27.

5. Brendan Gill, *Here at the New Yorker* (London: Michael Joseph, 1975), 123.

6. My source for the first performance is Mr. Robert E. Kimball, who kindly sent me the information.

7. Cole Porter, "Two Little Babes in the Wood" (New York: Harms, 1928), 9–10.

8. The White House denied that President Carter ever used the expression "three-Martini lunch." *Forbes*, 1 Nov. 1977, 34. See Deborah Rankin, "No More 'Free Lunch'?" *New York Times*, 6 Nov. 1977, F1: "Candidate Jimmy Carter signaled his intent to abolish what he called the '$50 Martini lunch' as part of his tax reform plan." Martinis and the expense account were linked in *Times Literary Supplement*, 26 Sept. 1958, 541: "It is yet another picture of capitalist economy run riot, when the expense account has clearly become a part of life, like baseball and Martinis."

9. *New York Times*, 18 Feb. 1978, 10. This was the Quotation of the Day.

Message three

Epigraph: Caroline Knapp, *Drinking: A Love Story* (New York: Dell, 1996), 47. Her emphasis.

1. And compare the members of the Century Club in New York. At its monthly black-tie dinner meetings, two bars are set up. One serves only Martinis and Manhattans, which are free. All other drinks, including water, must be ordered, and paid for, at the other.

2. The nickname is part of the picture. It was a class-linked one and for this reason was not common enough to enter dictionaries of American slang. "Martooni," on the other hand, appears in the 1967 edition of *Dictionary of American*

Slang, ed. Harold Wentworth and S. B. Flexner (New York: Thomas Y. Crowell), with the comment, "Fairly common jocular mispronunciation." Another nickname, about which I am uncertain, as regards its status, is "deep-dish olive pie." A waitress in Kurt Vonnegut Jr.'s novel called the Martini "breakfast of champions." *Breakfast of Champions* (New York: Dell, 1975), 194, 210. A good description of a Martini can be found on 196.

3. John Updike, *Too Far to Go* (New York: Fawcett Crest Paperback, 1979). The movie was shown on 12 Mar. 1979 at nine P.M. EST.

4. John J. O'Connor, "TV: Drama of Updike's Sad Couple," *New York Times,* 12 Mar. 1979. This reviewer did not consider the movie a soap opera but a "landmark in television programming."

5. *New York Review of Books* 28 (2 Apr. 1981): 37.

6. Donald Barthelme, "The Teachings of Don B.: A Yankee Way of Knowledge," in *Guilty Pleasures* (New York: Farrar, Straus, and Giroux, 1974), 53–62. Published earlier, probably in the *New Yorker,* but the vagueness of the front matter makes it impossible to tell.

7. Paul Fussell, *Class* (New York: Ballantine Books, 1984), 167.

8. John Leonard, *The Naked Martini* (New York: Delacorte, 1964), 44, 38, 225, 226, 228. In fairness to Leonard, I record his disavowal of the novel in his column "Private Lives," *New York Times,* 26 Mar. 1980: "a sickly thing in which too many words were wasted on how to mix a Martini without bruising the vermouth."

9. Willa Cather, *A Lost Lady,* in *Later Novels* (New York: Library of America, 1990), 25.

10. See the reproduction in Barnaby Conrad III, *The Martini: An Illustrated History of an American Classic* (San Francisco: Chronicle Books, 1995), 125, and his history of gin, 123–25.

11. "Written" applies to David Graham Phillips. See Simple Message 4 n. 5.

12. John R. Hale, "The First Performance," *Saturday Evening Post,* 10 Apr. 1909, 37, on faux pas on opening nights:

> When Rachel Crothers' "The Coming of Mrs. Patrick" was played . . . one of the situations was the mixing of a cocktail by Mrs. Patrick. . . . The ingredients furnished by the property-man made Mrs. Pat's cocktail look like black coffee, and the first-night death-watch, which in its sophistication could recognize a block away a Bronx, Martini or Manhattan cocktail by its color, of course, laughed, and again the critics took the episode as one of their texts for censure.

What cocktail was Mrs. Patrick mixing? I tried without success to locate the play. The reference is especially intriguing because a woman is mixing a cocktail. Cf. the reference to *Mrs. Beeton's Book of Household Management* below; and cf. Simple Message 4.

A twelfth reference to the Martini from the period 1900–1910 that is unmarked with respect to class is George Ade, "The Periodical Souse, the Never-Again Feeling, and the Ride on the Sprinkling Cart," in *People You Know* (New York, 1903), 20: "It was an actual Mystery to him that any one could dally with a Dry Martini while there was a Hydrant on every Corner." This is the on-again off-again drinker.

13. John Philip Sousa, *The Fifth String* (Indianapolis: Bowen-Merrill, 1902), 18. His emphasis.

14. Hidley Dhee, "A Daring Game," *Crescent*, 1 Aug. 1896, 11. This magazine was published by the Hamilton Athletic Club.

15. *Mrs. Beeton's Book of Household Management* (London: Ward, Lock, 1906), 1511. The recipe:

> Ingredients.—½ a wineglassful of good unsweetened gin, ½ a wineglassful of Italian vermouth, 6 drops of rock candy syrup, 12 drops of orange bitters, 1 small piece of lemon peel, crushed ice.
>
> Method—Half fill a tumbler with crushed ice, pour over it all the liquids, shake well, then strain into a glass, and serve with a small piece of lemon-peel floating on the surface.

16. Anistatia R. Miller and Jared M. Brown, *Shaken Not Stirred: A Celebration of the Martini* (New York: HarperPerennial, 1997), 34. The authors found the menu in the New York Public Library.

17. O. Henry, *The Gentle Grafter* (New York: Doubleday, Doran, 1908), 212–13, in the chapter or section called "Hostages to Momus." The book was first published in 1904.

18. Brand Whitlock, "Reform in the First," in *The Gold Brick* (New York: Hurst, 1910), 244. (The stories in this collection originally appeared in the *Saturday Evening Post,* the *American Magazine,* and *Ainslee's Magazine.*) In the first edition of this book I was misled by the ambiguity of "his" at the beginning of the quotation and connected the Martini with Nolan. I now think that it refers to Underwood.

19. G. H. Lorimer, *Jack Spurlock—Prodigal* (New York: Doubleday, Page, 1906), 24.

20. Now the Hotel Employees and Restaurant Employees International Union.

21. The recipe is practically identical to Jerry Thomas's recipe for the Martinez (1887). For Thomas, see "Historical Background of the Ambiguities" and "Theory, Method, and Bibliography."

MESSAGE FOUR

Epigraph: Russell Baker, *New York Times,* 28 Aug. 1979, A17.

1. Bernard DeVoto, *The Hour* (Boston: Houghton Mifflin, 1951), 35. Cf. the cartoon in the *New Yorker,* 24 Nov. 1956, 57: wife says to husband, "Oh dear! You mean it should have been four to one the *other* way?"

2. Telephone conversation, 19 Aug. 1997. A shrewd reader will note apparently contradictory evidence at Simple Message 3 n. 12 (Mrs. Patrick).

3. Cf. John Kobler, "Martinis cum Laude," in *Afternoon in the Attic* (New York: Dodd, Mead, 1949), 89. The head of a school for bartenders explains to the author that women are the reason for the proliferation of cocktails after Repeal: "Soon as they started drinking in bars, the good old stand-by—highball, beer, Martini—wouldn't do any more. They had to have their drinks fancy."

4. David Graham Phillips, *Susan Lenox: Her Fall and Rise* (New York: D. Appleton, 1917; reprint, Carbondale: Southern Illinois University Press, 1977). The novel was serialized and published posthumously. Phillips was murdered in 1911.

5. Ibid., 2:33–36. They also drink dry champagne, which she likes. She had begun to drink it on her first evening of prostitution (1:381, 384).

6. *New Yorker*, 15 Dec. 1986. The cartoon is by Reilly.

7. The Martini can be the woman's sexual gambit. See, in Ambiguity 2, the example of Mrs. Robinson (in the film *The Graduate*) and the strategy of M. F. K. Fisher.

8. Ernest Hemingway, *Across the River and into the Trees* (New York: Scribner's, 1950), 92.

9. Phillips, *Susan Lenox*, 2:98.

10. Ernest Hemingway, *The Sun Also Rises* (New York: Scribner's, 1926), 244.

11. M. F. K. Fisher, "To the Gibson and Beyond," *Atlantic*, Jan. 1949, 93; Bernard DeVoto, "For the Wayward and Beguiled" ("The Easy Chair"), *Harper's Magazine*, Dec. 1949, 68–71. These two articles led to a correspondence between Fisher and DeVoto that is to the student of the Martini what the correspondence of Elizabeth Barrett and Robert Browning or of John Quincy and Abigail Adams is to scholars in other fields. Alas, the Fisher-DeVoto correspondence has vanished. It cannot be located among DeVoto's papers in the archives of the Stanford University library, and Fisher had no record of it.

MESSAGE FIVE

Epigraph: Ernest Hemingway, "The Denunciation" (1938), in *The Fifth Column and Four Stories of the Spanish Civil War* (New York: Scribner's, 1969), 95.

1. *New York Times*, 22 Mar. 1978.

2. Bernard DeVoto, *The Hour* (Boston: Houghton Mifflin, 1951), 28–29. "Campground" is a metonymy for revivalist meeting.

3. Ibid., 43. Cf. the function of the Martini in John Berryman, *77 Dream Songs* (New York: Farrar, Straus, 1964), song no. 55.

4. F. Scott Fitzgerald, "The Rich Boy," in *All the Sad Young Men* (New York: Scribner's, 1926), 207.

5. *An Evening Wasted with Tom Lehrer*, Reprise 6199 (1959).

MESSAGE SIX

Epigraph: J. D. Salinger, "A Perfect Day for Bananafish," in *Nine Stories* (Boston: Little, Brown, 1953), 15. The story originally appeared in the *New Yorker*, 31 Jan. 1948, 21–25.

1. Kay Thompson, *Eloise* (New York: Simon and Schuster, 1955), 51.

2. The information in this paragraph was given me by Mr. Penn Holberd, an undergraduate member of the Owl Club at the time (1979 or 1980).

3. Theodore Dreiser, *An American Tragedy*, vol. 1 (New York, 1925), 55–56, 54.

4. Gerald Clarke, *Capote: A Biography* (New York: Simon and Schuster, 1988), 93. Clarke adds, "It was the first of many she was to share with him during the next few years."

5. Patrick Dennis (Edward Everett Tanner), *Auntie Mame* (New York: Vanguard, 1955), 24.

6. Jerome Lawrence and Robert E. Lee, *Auntie Mame* (New York: Vanguard, 1957), 39.

7. Consider also the child-adult opposition in Martini cartoons: e.g., Robert Herzbrun, *The Perfect Martini Book* (New York: Harcourt Brace Jovanovich, 1979), 76 and 86; *New Yorker*, 3 Apr. 1971, 44.

8. *The Best of Roald Dahl* (New York: Vintage Books, 1978), 239.

9. J. D. Salinger, *The Catcher in the Rye* (Boston: Little, Brown, 1951), chap. 19.

10. J. D. Salinger, *Franny and Zooey* (Boston: Little, Brown, 1961), 12–13, for the Martini scene. They order a second round on 15–16. The story "Franny" was originally published in the *New Yorker*, 29 Jan. 1955, 24–32, 35–43 (page numbers differ as between city and out-of-town editions).

MESSAGE SEVEN

Epigraph: Frank Zachary, "H$_2$Ode," *New Yorker*, 14 May 1979, 44.

1. For the 1920s, see Frederick Lewis Allen, *Only Yesterday: An Informal History of the Nineteen Twenties* (New York: Perennial Library, 1964), 211: "well-born damsels with one foot on the brass rail, tossing off Martinis."

For the 1930s, see advertisement by the General Trading Company in *Illustrated London News*, Sept. 1978, 76: "Have a martini in this Swedish glass of true 1930 design." Jeffrey Simpson, "A Skyline View," *Architectural Digest* 46 (Nov. 1989): 264–69: "The mood of Art Deco elegant nonchalance only lacks Fred Astaire and Ginger Rogers and a chrome martini shaker." Cf. also Claes Oldenburg, quoted in the conclusion to this book.

It is generally held that the 1940s was the decade in which the Martini became truly dry. See John Doxat, *Stirred—Not Shaken: The Dry Martini* (London: Hutchinson Benham, 1976), 35, and Donald J. Gonzales, "Crisis at the Cocktail Hour," *Saturday Review*, 15 Nov. 1975, 47, quoting Harold J. Grossman, *Guide to Wines, Spirits, and Beers* (New York: Scribner's, 1974).

As for the 1950s, see Stephen Holden, "Golden Girl of Vice K.O.'s Oleo Heir," *New York Times*, 18 July 1997, C16, on the 1997 film *Cafe Society* (about the 1952 sex scandal involving Mickey Jelke): "endless Martinis" contribute to the success of a "rare 50's period piece that gets it right." David Schiff, "Music," *Atlantic Monthly*, Sept. 1995, on a recording of Pierre Boulez' "Marteau sans maître": "Heard today, it might seem quintessentially fifties—a vodka martini set to music." For images of the Martini in the 1950s, see Max Rudin, "'There Is Something about a Martini,'" *American Heritage* 48, no. 4 (July–Aug. 1997): 46 (managers at Georgia-Pacific), and Gretchen Edgren, *The Playboy Book: Forty Years,* ed. Murray Fisher (Santa Monica, Calif.: General Publishing Group, 1994), 36–37.

Finally, for the 1960s: Bones Jackson, "Style and the Single Drinker," *Boston,* Aug. 1978, 66: "You want to drink something that won't embarrass you. In the fifties and sixties in New York, the martini was that drink." Cf. Jerry Della Femina, "The Hey-Day of the Three-Martini Lunch," *New York Times Magazine,* 28 Oct. 1989, 22.

2. Joan Kron, "Syrie Maugham Style Comes Ghosting Back," *New York Times,* 1 Dec. 1977, 49.

3. Michael Korda, "The Drink Date Dynamics," *New York Times,* 2 Nov. 1977, 21.

4. "Where Has All the Gin Gone?" *Forbes,* 1 Nov. 1977, 34. Cf. Jefferson Morgan, "Whatever Happened to the Martini?" *Bon Appetit,* Oct. 1978, 73–74.

5. Sarah Bradford, *The Englishman's Wine: The Story of Port* (London: St. Martin's, 1969), 98.

6. *New Yorker,* 18 July 1964, 20.

7. *Liquor Handbook 1978* (New York: Gavin-Jobson Associates, 1978), 248, 256.

8. I think that this is also the conclusion of my one planned attempt at empirical research. On 12 July 1978 my friend Norman B. Slocum, of Abt Associates, Inc., and I set out on what was to be a nine-hour Martini-tour of Boston and Cambridge bars. In the first few bars we both took notes, and these appear to corroborate the observations made in the preceding paragraph. On the way from Boston to Cambridge we were talking about Norm's boss, and the cabdriver, who seemed to be an acquaintance of Clark Abt, joined in the discussion. When he dropped us in Harvard Square, he said, "The big difference between Clark Abt and you guys is that Clark Abt wasn't sitting in a bar all afternoon."

9. Donald G. Smith, "To the Young, Vermouth Is a State," *Wall Street Journal,* 9 Dec. 1985, sec. 1, p. 24.

10. Loudon Wainwright, "Faces Passed," *New York Times Magazine,* 18 Dec. 1977, 45.

THE SIMPLE MESSAGES RECONSIDERED

1. William Grimes, *Straight Up or On the Rocks: A Cultural History of American Drink* (New York: Simon and Schuster, 1993), 31.

2. Max Rudin, "'There Is Something about a Martini,'" *American Heritage* 48, no. 4 (July–Aug. 1997): 32–51, 43.

3. E.g., the one reprinted by Barnaby Conrad III, *The Martini: An Illustrated History of an American Classic* (San Francisco: Chronicle Books, 1995), 94.

4. E.g., Jean Baudrillard, *America,* trans. Chris Turner (London: Verso, 1988), 28: "This [America] is the only country which gives you the opportunity to be so brutally naive: things, faces, skies, and deserts are expected to be simply what they are. This is the land of the 'just as it is.'"

5. Conrad, *Martini,* 97, 99.

AMBIGUITY ONE

1. Ernest Hemingway, *A Farewell to Arms* (New York: Scribner's, 1969), 245.

2. Sinclair Lewis, *Babbitt* (New York: New American Library, 1950), 85–86.

3. Sidney Petrie and R. B. Stone, *Martinis and Whipped Cream: The New Carbo-Cal Way to Lose Weight and Stay Slim* (West Nyack, N.Y.: Parker, 1966), 1–2.

4. George L. Herter and Berthe E. Herter, *Bull Cook and Authentic Historical Recipes and Practices* (Waseca, Minn.: published privately, 1969), 359.

5. M. F. K. Fisher, "To the Gibson and Beyond," *Atlantic,* Jan. 1949, 93.

6. Conrad Aiken, "Another Lycidas," in *Collected Poems,* 2d ed. (New York: Oxford University Press, 1970), 939, 943.

7. John Thomas, *Dry Martini: A Gentleman Turns to Love* (1926; reprint, Carbondale: Southern Illinois University Press, 1974), 250.

8. Jack London, *Burning Daylight* (New York: Macmillan, 1910), 5, 125.

9. Ibid., 132, 163–64.

10. Ibid., 210, 244, 275, 307.

11. Ibid., 308, 328.

12. *New Yorker,* 22 Oct. 1973, 142; 27 Nov. 1971, 89; 13 June 1977, 40; 18 Sept. 1978, 44; 23 Oct. 1978, 46.

13. John Doxat, *Stirred—Not Shaken: The Dry Martini* (London: Hutchinson Benham, 1976), 23.

14. Baba Erlanger and Daren Pierce, *The Compleat Martini Cookbook* (n.p.: Random Thoughts, 1957); Jane Trahey (Baba Erlanger) and Daren Pierce, *Son of the Martini Cookbook* (New York: Clovis, 1967). The quotation is from the preface to the latter.

15. Charles Jackson, *The Lost Weekend* (New York: Farrar and Rinehart, 1944), 29. Cf. *The Lost Weekend* (a Paramount Picture), screenplay by Charles Brackett and Billy Wilder, copyright 1945, in *Best Film Plays—1945*, ed. John Gassner and Dudley Nichols (New York: Crown, 1946), 35: "DON (*a little stiffly*). One more gin vermouth." Elsewhere, however, as in the novel, he is drinking whiskey.

16. John F. Murray, "O'Phelan Drinking," *New Yorker*, 3 Oct. 1977, 41.

17. Helen McCloy, *Alias Basil Willing* (New York: Walter J. Black, 1951), 85.

18. Cf. Dr. Percival in Graham Greene, *The Human Factor* (New York: Simon and Schuster, 1978), who takes it upon himself to murder, by poison, one Davis, an imagined security leak in the Secret Service. Dr. Percival is a Martini-drinker (36, 263). The innocent Davis is fond of port. The hero of the novel, Castle, drinks Scotch (217). When Daintry, the security officer, begins to fall into a sort of moral gloom over the death of Davis, he uncharacteristically drinks three Martinis at lunch and thinks of Dr. Percival.

19. *New York Times*, 14 Sept. 1997, 50.

20. Ryne Duren, "Alcoholic Pitcher's Last Game (and Almost Last Day of Life)," *New York Times*, 14 May 1978, sec. 5, p. 2.

21. The Martini goes with football, at least Ivy League football (see the quotations from Smith and Wainwright in Simple Message 7), but not with baseball, no matter how American baseball may be (cf. Simple Message 2 n. 8). There must be some social difference between the two sports that determines the Martini's affinity for one but not the other.

22. Roger Angell, *The Summer Game* (New York: Popular Library, 1972), 100.

AMBIGUITY TWO

1. John Leonard, *The Naked Martini* (New York: Delacorte, 1964), 149–50.

2. John Dos Passos, *Manhattan Transfer* (New York: Harper and Brothers, 1925), 373–74. All the ellipses are Dos Passos's.

3. Ernest Hemingway, *Across the River and into the Trees* (New York: Scribner's, 1950), 82–83.

4. Evelyn Waugh, *Brideshead Revisited: The Sacred and Profane Memories of Captain Charles Ryder* (Boston: Little, Brown, 1945), 274. Yes, it could be the weaker English form of the Martini known as "Gin 'n It."

5. F. Scott Fitzgerald, *The Beautiful and the Damned* (New York: Scribner's, 1922), 86. With the absinthe, cf. Pernod, n. 22 below. Elsewhere in this novel, which is awash with liquor, Fitzgerald almost always says "cocktail" and does not specify the type.

6. E.g., in *Newsweek*, 22 Oct. 1979.

7. M. F. K. Fisher, *An Alphabet for Gourmets*, in *The Art of Eating* (New York: Vintage Books, 1976), 708. Cf. Robert Lowell, "Homecoming," in *Day by Day* (New York: Farrar, Straus, and Giroux, 1977), 11: "we made it/on . . . martinis."

8. I have not been able to find this poem in the works of Dorothy Parker.

9. *New York Times,* 29 Aug. 1979, C11. In "The Sorrows of Gin," the television adaptation of John Cheever's short story, Mr. Lawton compared his wife's kisses to a Martini. Shown on WNET-TV in New York on 24 Oct. 1979 at nine P.M. The story is in *The Stories of John Cheever* (New York: Alfred A. Knopf, 1978), 198–209.

10. Renata Adler, *Speedboat* (New York: Random House, 1976), 137–38.

11. Dorothy Parker, "Dusk before Fireworks," in *The Collected Stories of Dorothy Parker* (New York: Random House, 1942), 282–83.

12. Sara Davidson, *Loose Change* (New York: Pocket Books, 1978), 164–65.

13. Leonard, *Naked Martini,* 68; Bernard DeVoto, "For the Wayward and Beguiled" ("The Easy Chair"), *Harper's Magazine,* Dec. 1949, 68. In DeVoto's *The Hour,* 29, the phrase became "a wife (or some other charming woman) of attuned impulse." In other words, either the romantic or the conjugal Martini.

14. See Figure 4. Compare *New Yorker,* 5 Aug. 1967, 28–29; 4 Feb. 1967, 35; 31 May 1969, 85; 8 Nov. 1969, 64; 29 Nov. 1976, 37.

15. I am grateful to Carol Capeci of J. Walter Thompson for her attempts to locate the original of this advertisement. Unfortunately for me, she could not find it, nor could she supply any information about where or when it was published. I have the tearsheet that appears in the plate simply because someone (I do not remember who) sent it to me (without any reference) in the 1980s.

16. *New Yorker,* 11 Mar. 1985, 45; 24 Mar. 1986, 41; 24 June 1991, 35. Cf. 31 July 1989, 75: a running Martini greets the tired husband as he returns home (no caption). Cf. also the observations of Barbara Holland, *Endangered Pleasures: In Defense of Naps, Bacon, Martinis, Profanity, and Other Indulgences* (Boston: Little, Brown, 1995), 41:

> In the olden days, the returning breadwinner was greeted by his wife at the door with a perfectly chilled martini; sometimes, at least in cartoons, she positively rushed down the front walk with it. It restored his soul, loosened his tightly coiled nerves, and punctuated the day, closing off the business portion and ushering in the evening.
>
> After a few happy decades of this, she went out and got a job, and he was greeted at the door by a basket of dirty laundry instead. It's just not the same.

Holland proceeds to recommend a Martini in a bar. The conjugal Martini reverts to the Martini-of-the-relationship in her vision.

17. On which see R. B. Harwell, *The Mint Julep* (Charlottesville: University Press of Virginia, 1975).

18. DeVoto's "For the Wayward and Beguiled" is cited above in n. 13.

19. Peter Conrad, "The Man with the X-Ray Eye," *Times Literary Supplement,* 22 Aug. 1997, 18 (review of Patrick McGilligan, *Fritz Lang: The Nature of the Beast* [London: Faber, 1997]).

20. Dr. Peter Knapp, mentioned above in Simple Message 3, always had a small bowl of raw carrots and a small bowl of unsalted peanuts. Caroline Knapp, *Drinking: A Love Story* (New York: Dell, 1996), 38.

21. E. M. Jellinek, "The Symbolism of Drinking: A Culture-Historical Approach," *Journal of Studies on Alcohol* 38 (1977): 852–66.

22. Thévenot may represent self-parody on the part of Buñuel. He gives his own lecture on Martini-mixing in his autobiography, *My Last Sigh* (New York: Vintage Books, 1983), 44–45. A detail in the scene I have discussed (Thévenot says that you can add a drop of Pernod as they did in the United States in the 1930s) is found in the autobiography (but it is the 1940s); and there are other points of convergence.

AMBIGUITY THREE

1. Robert Herzbrun, *The Perfect Martini Book* (New York: Harcourt Brace Jovanovich, 1979). Cf. Anthony Spinazzola, "The Perfect, Perfect Martini," *Boston Sunday Globe,* 20 Nov. 1966; F. S. Frail, "In Search of the Perfect Martini," *Savor* (supplement to *Boston Phoenix*), 29 May 1979, 6.

2. *New Yorker,* 8 Jan. 1979, 53.

3. Peter C. Hotton, "Polishing off the Floors. . . ," *Boston Globe,* 27 Oct. 1978, 26.

4. For the Gordon's and Seagram's campaigns, see "The New Look in Martinis," *Liquor Store,* Jan. 1968. Compare the Beefeater advertisement that began to appear about a decade later (e.g., *New York Times,* 22 Oct. 1979, A11). It is entitled "Why We Will Never Tell You How to Make a Beefeater Martini." The theme of the advertisement is the relativism of tastes in the Martini. The cyclical nature of such themes in gin advertising is further proof that the Martini's associations constitute a synchronous system.

5. *Time,* 19 Oct. 1959, 31, with a photograph of the "dillytini."

6. *New Yorker,* 16 Dec. 1977, 28.

7. George A. Macomber, "Rambling Notes on the Cambridge Trust Company, or Tales of a Wayside Bank," Cambridge Historical Society *Proceedings* 41 (1967–69): 48. For the gourmet who frowns upon cocktails but permits a Martini, cf. Andre L. Simon, *The Gourmet's Week-End Book* (London: Seeley Service, 1952), 91, who states that "cocktails are an abomination" but goes on to say that there is no real harm in a Martini. Craig Claiborne served Martinis to his guests. See *New York Times,* 31 Jan. 1979, C1.

8. *New Yorker,* 7 Nov. 1956, 136.

9. "Martini Heresy," *Life,* 10 Dec. 1951, 81–82.

10. From an unpublished essay by Paul Nyeland on the L.M.S.O. or O. Society. His essay is also the source of the rest of my information on the society.

AMBIGUITY FOUR

1. Bernard DeVoto, *The Hour* (Boston: Houghton Mifflin, 1951), 39.

2. Robin Maugham, *Conversations with Willie: Recollections of W. Somerset Maugham* (New York: Simon and Schuster, 1978), 112.

3. Leo Engel, *American and Other Drinks* (London, 1880), 70.

4. A. S. Crockett, *The Old Waldorf-Astoria Bar Book* (New York: Dodd, Mead, 1934), 59–60.

5. I was able to obtain a copy of this letter from the archives of the American Antiquarian Society (Worcester, Mass.) through the kindness of Mr. Marcus A. McCorison, director and librarian, and Mr. William L. Joyce, curator of manuscripts. The latter wrote to me on 31 Jan. 1978, "According to a letter, dated May 1951, to the editors of *Harper's Magazine,* Clarence Brigham turned over all of his

notes to Bernard DeVoto after learning that DeVoto intended to write a history of the cocktail." These notes seem to have disappeared. Mrs. DeVoto has told me that she has no knowledge of them, and despite the best efforts of Professor Wallace Stegner and Mr. Florian Shasky, chief of the Department of Special Collections, the notes could not be found in the DeVoto papers in the Stanford University Libraries.

6. Berton Roueche, *The Neutral Spirit: A Portrait of Alcohol* (Boston: Little, Brown, 1960), 55.

7. Giorgio Lolli, Howard W. Haggard, and Leon A. Greenberg, "The Absorption of Alcohol with Special Reference to Its Influence on the Concentration of Alcohol Appearing in the Blood," *Quarterly Journal of Studies on Alcohol* 1 (1941): 684–726; Giorgio Lolli, Rodolfo Nencini, and Rafaello Misiti, "Effects of Two Alcoholic Beverages on the Electroencephalographic and Electromyographic Tracings of Healthy Men," *Quarterly Journal of Studies on Alcohol* 25 (1964): 451–58.

8. *New Yorker,* 18 Mar. 1967, 173.

9. W. H. Auden, from "Symmetries and Asymmetries," in *Collected Poems,* ed. Edward Mendelson (Franklin Center, Pa.: Franklin Library, 1976), 551. The editor tentatively dates the poem to 1963–64.

10. George Burns, *Wisdom of the 90s* (New York: G. P. Putnam's Sons, 1993), 80, 83. Photographs of Burns with cigar and with Martini on 68.

11. *New Yorker,* 6 Jan. 1997, 61.

12. *Esquire,* June 1986, 349.

13. Barnaby Conrad, *The Cigar* (San Francisco: Chronicle Books, 1996).

14. Kina Lillet is the same thing as the Lillet sold in the United States. It is a blend of wines flavored with various herbals, thus a sort of vermouth.

15. Ian Fleming, *Casino Royale* (London: Jonathan Cape, 1953), 60–61, 69–70.

16. *People,* 5 June 1978, 94.

17. Ernest Hemingway, *Across the River and into the Trees* (New York: Scribner's, 1950), 35.

18. Ernest Hemingway, *Islands in the Stream* (New York: Scribner's, 1970). For Martinis, see 51 and probably elsewhere.

19. John Doxat, *Stirred—Not Shaken: The Dry Martini* (London: Hutchinson Benham, 1976), 128.

20. With Leiter: *Thunderball* (New York: Viking, 1961), 122; also *Live and Let Die* (New York: Macmillan, 1955), 7–8, where Fleming writes, "They drank the cold, hard drink appreciatively"; cf. 36 and 90. With M.: *Moonraker* (New York: Macmillan, 1955), 30 (but M. is drinking whiskey and soda). With Solitaire: *Live and Let Die,* 212. With Tiffany Case: *Diamonds Are Forever* (New York: Macmillan, 1956), in *More Gilt-Edged Bonds* (New York: Macmillan, 1965), 513; other Martinis on 492, 507, 521, 558, 573, 576, 626. These passages are worth study. Note especially 492, where the Martinis appear in the company of caviar and smoked-salmon canapés. As I argued at the beginning of Ambiguity 1, the Martini is the drink of opulence.

21. Dashiell Hammett, *The Thin Man* (New York: Alfred A. Knopf, 1934). The movie also appeared in 1934.

22. See Geoffrey O'Brien, *Hardboiled America: The Lurid Years of Paperbacks* (New York: Van Nostrand, 1981), 68–93, on Hammett as the pivotal figure in the history of "hardboiled" fiction.

23. Giorgio Lolli, *Social Drinking: How to Enjoy Drinking without Being Hurt by It* (Cleveland and New York: World, 1960), 92.

HISTORICAL BACKGROUND OF THE AMBIGUITIES

1. Roland Barthes, "Wine and Milk," in *Mythologies,* trans. A. Lavers (New York: Hill and Wang, 1972), 58–61.

2. Fernand Braudel, *Civilization and Capitalism: 15th–18th Century,* vol. 1, *The Structures of Everyday Life: The Limits of the Possible,* trans. Miriam Kochan and rev. Siân Reynolds (New York: Harper and Row, 1981), 243. The history of distillation and of the use of distilled alcohol is full of lacunae, and the majestic sweep of Braudel's gaze is hindered again and again when he comes to this subject (as he acknowledges: 243, 246, 247, 248). Even more damaging (and it is unacknowledged) to Braudel's discussion is the blurring, in this stretch of his narrative, of his thematic distinction between rich and poor, between the drinking habits of the privileged and the majority.

3. The earliest Greek source for distillation is Zosimus of Panopolis (in Upper Egypt) of the third or fourth century A.D. See George Sarton, *Introduction to the History of Science* (Baltimore: Williams and Wilkens, 1927), 339: "A book on beer-brewing is also ascribed to him." But Zosimus was not using distillation to produce alcohol. The earliest recipe for the preparation of alcohol appears in the first half of the twelfth century A.D. in a Latin treatise. See Sarton, 534, and R. J. Forbes, *A Short History of the Art of Distilling* (Leiden: E. J. Brill, 1970), 87–89. Neither did the Arabs use distillation for alcohol. See Sarton, vol. 2 (1931), 29, 408. The Arabs used distillation to make rose water and perfumes. See *The Encyclopaedia of Islam,* vol. 1 (1913), s.v. *alembic,* and vol. 2 (1927), s.v. *al-kīmiyā',* 1015. Helmust Arntz, *Weinbrenner: Die Geschichte vom Geist des Weines* (Stuttgart: Seewald Verlag, 1975), 211, believes that Europeans took over the technique of distillation from the Arabs. For a survey of the early history of distilling in Europe, see Arntz, 202–34, and also Forbes, 55–98.

4. "Makings for a Martini," *Consumer Reports,* Nov. 1960, 591–95.

5. But see Kingsley Amis, n. 79 below.

6. George R. Stewart, *American Ways of Life* (Garden City, N.Y.: Doubleday, 1954), 115–21; Gerald Carson, *The Social History of Bourbon: An Unhurried Account of Our Star-Spangled American Drink* (New York: Dodd, Mead, 1963), chaps. 1–3; Reay Tannahill, *Food in History* (New York: Stein and Day, 1973), 295–98.

7. Cited in previous note.

8. "Gin Comes out of the Bathtub," *Scientific American* 150, no. 3 (Mar. 1934): 156. The occasion of the article was the use of nickel and a nickel-chromium alloy in gin distilleries.

9. Sterling North and Carl Kroch, eds., *So Red the Nose, or Breath in the Afternoon* (New York: Farrar and Rhinehart, 1935), no pagination. The recipes submitted by Roberts, Dorothy Aldis, and E. Phillips Oppenheim were for Martinis. Aldis's garnish was a sprig of mint. Oppenheim instructed, "Shake *like hell,* and serve foaming in a fair-sized glass."

10. *Mida's National Register of Trade Marks: Spirituous [sic] and Malt Liquors and Wines,* 2 vols. (Chicago: Mida's Criterion, n.d.). On the card in the catalogue in Widener Library a date in the 1890s is given, with a question mark.

There are in the *Register* 203 pages of whiskey trademarks and 9 pages of gin trademarks. Vermouth trademarks do not appear, for the simple reason that vermouth was not yet being manufactured in the United States.

11. Stewart, *American Ways of Life*, 119.

12. I have not verified this quotation, which I have come across several times—e.g., in W. A. Craigie and J. R. Hulbert, eds., *Dictionary of American English on Historical Principles* (Chicago: University of Chicago Press, 1940), s.v. *cocktail*.

13. Henry Didimus, *New Orleans As I Found It* (New York, 1845), 25.

14. For a survey of etymologies, see H. L. Mencken, *The American Language*, suppl. 1 (New York: Alfred A. Knopf, 1945), 256–60.

15. Jerry Thomas, *How to Mix Drinks, or The Bon Vivant's Companion* (New York, 1862), 49. His emphasis.

16. William Terrington, *Cooling Cups and Dainty Drinks* (London and New York, 1869), 190. Cf., however, for the dinner hour, Patsy McDonough, *McDonough's Bar-keeper's Guide* (Rochester, N.Y., 1883), 5: "The Cocktail is a very popular drink. It is most frequently called for in the morning and just before dinner; it is sometimes taken as an appetizer; it is a welcome companion on fishing excursions and travelers often go provided with it on a railroad journey."

17. Carson, *Social History of Bourbon*, 63.

18. I have taken this quotation from R. B. Harwell, *The Mint Julep* (Charlottesville: University Press of Virginia, 1975), 21.

19. Henry Porter and George Roberts, *Cups and Their Customs* (London, 1863), 30. But the American cocktail also promised a kind of alcoholic tourism. The physician John Steinhauser wrote to his friend Richard Francis Burton in 1860 inviting him to "come with me and drink through America." "I'll drink mint-juleps, brandy-smashes, whisky-skies, gin-sling, cock-tail sherry, cobblers, rum-salads, streaks of lightning, morning glory, and it'll be a most interesting experiment—I want to see whether after a life of 3 or 4 months I can drink and eat myself to the level of the aborigines—like you." They made the trip. How much time they spent together is unclear. Steinhauser died soon, apparently of drink. See Edward Rice, *Captain Sir Richard Francis Burton: The Secret Agent Who Made the Pilgrimage to Mecca, Discovered the "Kama Sutra," and Brought the "Arabian Nights" to the West* (New York: Scribner's, 1990), 330–39.

20. Advertisement in Leo Engel, *American and Other Drinks* (London, 1880). Most of the seventy-three pages of this book were pirated from the first (1862) edition of Thomas, *How to Mix Drinks*.

21. *Boston Morning Post*, 18 June 1838, 2.

22. *Columbian Sentinel*, 13 June 1838, 2.

23. J. K. Paulding and W. I. Paulding, *Madmen All, or The Cure of Love*, in *American Comedies* (Philadelphia, 1847), 188. For "stone fence," see Craigie and Hulbert, eds., *Dictionary of American English*, and cf. Burning Daylight's "stone wall" (= Martini) in Ambiguity 1.

24. Cf. the barroom scene in Nathaniel Hawthorne, *The Blithedale Romance* (written 1851–52), chap. 21, in which the mixing of a gin cocktail is described. Hawthorne says that the younger class of customers preferred cocktails—that is, the cocktail, as in the passage from the *Nation* quoted in the text, is the new drink.

25. Oberto Spinola, *The Martini Museum of the History of Wine-Making*

(Turin: Martini and Rossi, n.d.), 36. Although Mr. Bruno Torti, the United States representative of Martini and Rossi, generously sent me information (which I shall cite below) on the manufacture of vermouth, he was deaf to my questions concerning the history of Martini and Rossi in the United States.

26. The Only William (A. William Schmidt), *The Flowing Bowl: When and What to Drink* (New York, 1892); *Cocktails: How to Make Them* (Providence, 1898), 9.

27. Thomas, *How to Mix Drinks* (1862), 51. The abbreviation do. = ditto.

28. O. H. Byron, *The Modern Bartender's Guide* (New York, 1884).

29. George J. Kappeler, *Modern American Drinks* (Akron, Ohio, 1895), 38. The recipe for the Martini concludes, "Add a maraschino cherry, if desired by customer."

30. William T. Boothby, *Cocktail Boothby's American Bartender* (San Francisco, 1891), recipe no. 27.

31. Cf. The Only William, *Flowing Bowl*, 118–19:

As we mention syrup or gum so often, we think it necessary to call your attention to the way of making and using it.

Take an enameled pot of about half a gallon; put in this one and a half quarts of water and two pounds of loaf-sugar; let this boil over a slow fire; stir now and then, and skim well; if too thick, add a little boiling water; and strain into a bottle. It ought to be kept in a cold place. Do not prepare too large quantities, as it is best to have it fresh.

Rock-candy gum is prepared in the same way. Cocktail gum should be absolutely white.

32. Jerry Thomas, *How to Mix Drinks*, 2d ed. (New York, 1887). I repeat: his Martini recipe appears for the first time in this edition. I have seen with my own eyes the 1876 edition of Jerry Thomas's manual (New York: Dick and Fitzgerald), 130 pp. It does not contain a recipe for the Martinez or the Martini or any similar drink in which gin and vermouth are combined. This 1876 edition appears to be a reprint of the first (1862) edition.

33. Harry Johnson, *New and Improved Illustrated Bartender's Manual, or How to Mix Drinks of the Present Style* (New York, 1888), 38. See Figure 6 for an illustration from this manual.

34. Harry W. Stiles, *The Chapin and Gore Manual* (Chicago, 1888), 21.

35. Henry J. Wehman, *Wehman's Bartender's Guide* (New York, 1891), 10.

36. C. F. Lawlor, *The Mixologist* (Cincinnati, 1895). The recipe concludes, "Add one imported cherry."

37. Thomas Stuart, *Stuart's Fancy Drinks and How to Mix Them* (New York, 1896), 21.

38. Charles Ranhofer, *The Epicurean* (Chicago, 1893), 1066.

39. Kappeler, *Modern American Drinks* (cited in n. 29 above).

40. Joseph L. Haywood, *Mixology: The Art of Preparing All Kinds of Drinks* (Wilmington, Del., 1898), 18. The recipe concludes, "Twist lemon peel on top maraschino cherry."

41. *Cocktails: How to Make Them* (cited in n. 26 above).

42. [Frederic Lawrence Knowles], *The Cocktail Book: A Sideboard Manual for Gentlemen* (Boston: L. C. Page, 1900), 18–19. He gives two Martini recipes,

one of which calls for "half a teaspoonful sherry," as does one of the Martini recipes in *Cocktails: How to Make Them.*

43. Tim Daly, *Daly's Bartender's Encyclopedia* (Worcester, Mass.: published privately, 1903), 69, where I assume that "vermuth" means sweet vermouth (the recipe calls for Tom gin). But in the recipe on 47 entitled "Bottle of Martini Cocktail," "French vermuth" is called for, and Daly states, "This is supposed to be a very dry cocktail." The gin, however, is still the sweet Tom gin.

44. J. F. Hansman wrote to me on 21 Dec. 1981 that the earliest recipe for a "dry Martini" is in 1910, but he did not give me the reference. There are references to the dry Martini in literature in 1902 (Sousa), 1903 (Ade), and Lorimer (1906). See Simple Message 3 nn. 13, 12, and 19.

45. The 1876 edition of Thomas (New York: Dick and Fitzgerald) does not contain a recipe for the Martinez or Martini.

46. Paul E. Lowe, *Drinks As They Are Mixed* (Chicago: Frederick J. Drake, 1904), 21. Lawlor and Stuart are cited in nn. 36 and 37 above.

47. O. Henry, *The Gentle Grafter* (1904; reprint, New York: Doubleday, Doran, 1908), 212–13. Quoted in Simple Message 3.

48. Stiles, *Chapin and Gore Manual,* at the back of the book (no pagination), under the heading, "A DISTINCT DRINK FOR EACH AND EVERY DAY THROUGH-OUT THE YEAR, COMPILED AND ARRANGED IN STRICT ACCORD WITH THE SEASON."

49. "Don't Say Martini, Say Martinez," *Oakland Tribune,* 22 Aug. 1965, 19, 22. See also Peter Tamony, "Martini Cocktail," *Western Folklore* 26 (1967): 125–26.

50. Kendall Banning, *The Squire's Recipes* (Chicago: Brothers of the Book, 1912), no pagination.

51. George L. Herter and Berthe E. Herter, *Bull Cook and Authentic Historical Recipes and Practices* (Waseca, Minn.: published privately, 1969), 358–59, fabricated the invention of the Martini by the composer J. P. Schwarzendorf, who adopted the name "Martini" when he immigrated to France, perhaps to create confusion with the Italian composer of the same name. The Herters think that it was his "nickname."

52. Stiles, *Chapin and Gore Manual* (cited in n. 34 above).

53. Stuart, *Stuart's Fancy Drinks* (cited in n. 37 above).

54. "The Golden Age of Booze," in *Valentine's Manual of Old New York,* new series, no. 7 (1923): 134.

55. The mathematics can be found in David A. Embury, *The Fine Art of Mixing Drinks* (Garden City, N.Y.: Dolphin Books, 1961), 120.

56. Thus in "A Drink with Something in It," in *The Primrose Path* (New York: Simon and Schuster, 1935), 102, Ogden Nash describes a Martini as "yellow." Cf. John Thomas, *Dry Martini: A Gentleman Turns to Love* (1926; reprint, Carbondale: Southern Illinois University Press, 1974), 37: "a fragrant amber." Cf. the advertisements reprinted in Barnaby Conrad III, *The Martini: An Illustrated History of an American Classic* (San Francisco: Chronicle Books, 1995), 105, 125. Curiously, in the 1950s, in Ian Fleming, *Casino Royale* (London: Jonathan Cape, 1953), 60–61 (quoted in Ambiguity 4), one still finds "the pale golden drink."

57. The information in this paragraph comes from an essay, unpublished so far as I know, sent me by Mr. Bruno Torti, the United States representative of

Martini and Rossi. The clarity of the vermouth, it should be noted, was the last of the elements of the Martini to attain perfection.

58. Bernard DeVoto, *The Hour* (Boston: Houghton Mifflin, 1951), 42.

59. Perrin C. Galpin, ed., *Hugh Gibson, 1833–1954: Extracts from His Letters and Anecdotes from His Friends* (New York: Belgian American Educational Foundation, 1956), 28, tells the story of the origin of the Gibson Martini. Hugh Gibson was one of a group stationed at the State Department in the old building on Pennsylvania Avenue. They walked to the Metropolitan Club after work each day. Gibson could not handle the second and third drinks his companions ordered, "and at the same time," he said, "I did not want to ruin the party for the rest of the boys, so I arranged with the bartender to fill my glass with plain water on the second and all later rounds. As he did not want to confound my drink of plain water with the others he got into the habit of placing a pickled, baby onion in it." His colleagues discovered that Gibson could drink with no inebriating effects and began to order the "Gibson." For them, the bartender made the drink with almost all gin and very little vermouth—and the pickled baby onion. I am grateful to Lee A. Ghajar for this material. A similar story is told concerning Charles Dana Gibson (1867–1944), the illustrator after whom the Gibson Girl was named. See Anistatia R. Miller and Jared M. Brown, *Shaken Not Stirred: A Celebration of the Martini* (New York: HarperPerennial, 1997), 36, and, for other stories about the origin of the Gibson, Conrad, *Martini*, 117–18.

60. Braudel, *Civilization and Capitalism* (cited in n. 2 above), 241.

61. Edward R. Emerson, *Beverages Past and Present,* vol. 2 (New York: G. P. Putnam's Sons, 1908), 480.

62. A. S. Crockett, *Peacocks on Parade* (New York: Sears, 1931), 87–88.

63. *The Saloon in the Home,* comp. Ridgely Hunt and George S. Chappell (New York: Coward-McCann, 1930).

64. Jack London, *John Barleycorn* (New York: Century, 1913), 267: "I was never interested enough in cocktails to know how they were made. So I got a bartender in Oakland to make them in bulk and ship them to me."

65. E.g., *Puck,* 28 Nov. 1894, 238. Cf. Figure 3. My source for the date is *Heublein at 100* (Farmington, Conn.: Heublein, n.d.), no pagination. From this source and from correspondence with Mr. Thomas G. Cockerill, director of corporate communications at Heublein, I learn that the Martini played a part in the invention of the bottled cocktail. G. F. Heublein and Bro. were grocers and caterers in Hartford. When the Connecticut Governor's Foot Guards planned an outing, they ordered a gallon of Martinis and a gallon of Manhattans. On the weekend of the event, it rained, and it rained again the following weekend. The cocktails were forgotten until some later time when they were found in storage. The fortunate disobedience of the Heublein employees who had been ordered to throw them out revealed that the cocktails were as good as ever. The Heublein brothers then began to purvey bottled cocktails to the carriage trade that stopped at their store, and by the turn of the century these were the mainstay of their business. There is no documentary or other primary evidence for this story, but Mr. Cockerill has written me that it belongs to the traditional, oral history of Heublein.

66. The letter, which appeared, I believe, in *Town Topics: The Journal of Society,* runs as follows:

Did you get the Heublein Club Cocktails Garrie sent you? (Just to mention them makes me thirsty!) You will remember my modest little request to Tom to send me the whole outfit for Christmas? Did I tell you that he amiably obeyed? Well, that stock being decidedly depleted, you may figure to yourself my exceeding joy when two dozen little half-pint flasks of the delicious mixture greeted my waking eyes one recent morning! Tommy had bribed Babette to arrange them on the mantel while I slumbered, and a goodly show they made, I assure you! There were Tom Gins and Hollands, Vermouths, Manhattans, Martinis, and whiskies—not a single variety missing—and I found it difficult to choose which one to commence the cheerful day on!

I selected the vermouth, however, put outside the window while I was dressing, and there it was, refreshingly cold and bracing when I had adjusted my last frill and hairpin.

What a bother it would have been to stop to make it, or to ring for one to be served, thus giving one's indecorous thirst away to the whole household! I drank cordially to the health of Tommy, and "another one"—reverently—to the genius Heublein, who invented the stunning stuff.

I suppose you would only be contented with the quart bottles; but Mariquita and I find the little half-pints hold two very sizable drinks, and we have a fine scheme for the flasks. They are jolly little glass affairs, of the pudgy shape of the Stein wine bottles, and it occurred to us what pretty things they would be, decorated. No sooner suggested than tried, and we have gilded and silvered and bronzed them, and I have painted flowers, and Mariquita ideal heads, till we have quite an exhibit. We shall tie big satin bows on the handles, and utilize them on gift days, and I'm not sure but we'll bestow one upon you at Easter, if you think you are nice enough to deserve one. But I don't know, it would be just like you to kick because it's empty!

Au revoir, Auntie is calling me to lunch, and if I do not hasten she will fancy the cold capon is growing warm, and the Ruinart losing its fine frappé.

Your very devoted,

HONORA.

67. Cf. McDonough, *McDonough's Bar-keeper's Guide* (cited in n. 16 above).

68. Alec Waugh, *Wines and Spirits* (New York: Time-Life Books, 1968), 33.

69. She told me the story in Cambridge in the fall of 1977.

70. I heard about the turkey-carving in conversation with Professor Frank Freidel of Harvard University in 1977.

71. Costigan's screenplay was based on Joseph P. Lash, *Eleanor and Franklin* (New York: W. W. Norton, 1971), but incorporated material from other sources as well.

72. Frank Freidel, *Franklin D. Roosevelt: Launching the New Deal* (Boston: Little, Brown, 1973), 281.

73. The purpose of this study is to chart the symbolism and mythology of the Martini, not to write its history; but if the reader wishes to know what sort of Martinis came out of that silver shaker, here is the historical truth: In general, one batch of Roosevelt's Martinis was never like another. The only uniformity

was in the relative amounts of gin and vermouth. The proportion of the latter to the former could reach seven to one, and sometimes he used both sweet and dry. Roosevelt saw no reason not to add fruit juice to Martinis, or Pernod, or Anisette. Grace Tully, one of Roosevelt's secretaries and one of the "children," tells in her memoirs that Roosevelt once absent-mindedly made a Martini of aquavit instead of gin. In fairness, it must be added that on this occasion even Roosevelt felt that he had erred. See Grace Tully, *F.D.R., My Boss* (New York: Scribner's, 1949), 23. For sweet and dry vermouth in the Martini, see Charles E. Bohlen, *Witness to History: 1929–1969* (New York: W. W. Norton, 1973), 143. For fruit juice in the Martini, see S. I. Rosenman, *Working with Roosevelt* (New York: Da Capo, 1972), 150. Franklin D. Roosevelt Jr., in a letter of 12 Oct. 1971 to Mr. James Whitehead, curator of the Franklin D. Roosevelt Library at Hyde Park, N.Y., states, "He also made a very dry martini, but most of the family told him that he ruined it by adding a few drops of Anisette." Professor Frank Freidel, in a letter to me of 28 Sept. 1977, described Roosevelt's cocktails as "horrendous" and added, "I use the word horrendous deliberately." The evidence for the Roosevelt Martini provided by William O. Douglas, *Go East Young Man: The Early Years: The Autobiography of William O. Douglas* (New York: Random House, 1974), 334, is strangely anomalous. Douglas has Roosevelt drinking the classic dry Martini.

74. It seems unnecessary to give documentary evidence for the bizarre practices mentioned in this paragraph. I regret to say that I have either seen them myself or have heard about them from reliable eyewitnesses.

75. *New York Times Magazine*, 6 Apr. 1952, 41. This article lists several of the techniques practiced by the fetishist of dryness.

76. See the photograph of the box in Conrad, *Martini*, 38.

77. Letter to the editor of the *Boston Sunday Globe*, 25 Dec. 1966.

78. In the 1970s, Seagram's advertising associated the Martini with the *sake* ceremony, showing a kimono-clad Japanese woman kneeling beside a cocktail tray and stirring Martinis in a pitcher.

79. In the opening scene of T. S. Eliot's *The Cocktail Party* (1950), the Unidentified Guest, offered cocktails or whiskey, chooses straight gin with a drop of water. The choice increases the strangeness of this Stranger, I think. But Kingsley Amis, *Every Day Drinking* (London: Hutchinson, 1983), 10, recommends gin and water, though with lemon and ice. After a period of abstention, his first drink "was a glass of plain Gordon's gin and water." He adds, "One thing it did for me was confirm my judgement that when it comes to drinking gin, there's no other decent way." Is Amis at all typical? If so, Eliot's Stranger is not as strange as I say.

CONCLUSION

1. Claes Oldenburg, *Multiples in Retrospect: 1964–1990* (New York: Rizzoli, 1991), 154.

2. Ibid., 132. Sixty-five contradicts the figure (fifty) given on 154.

3. Ibid., 137.

THEORY, METHOD, AND BIBLIOGRAPHY

1. Probably the proportion of pages on drinking to pages on food in Polly Wiessner and Wulf Schifenhövel, eds., *Food and the Status Quest: An Interdisci-*

plinary Perspective (Providence, R.I.: Berghahn Books, 1996), is indicative, even if this collection of essays is addressed to food. See the index, s.v. *drinking*.

2. Henry Porter and George Roberts, *Cups and Their Customs* (London, 1863), iii–iv. Their emphasis.

3. Some examples: Maurice Healy, *Stay Me with Flagons* (London: M. Joseph, 1949); Cyril Ray, ed., *The Compleat Imbiber*, 12 vols. (London: Putnam, 1956–71); William Terrington, *Cooling Cups and Dainty Drinks* (London and New York, 1869). Such writing becomes, at its most thorough, encyclopedic, as in John Doxat, *Drinks and Drinking* (London: Hutchinson Benham, 1971). For a brilliant handling and, occasionally, parody of the genre, see Kingsley Amis, *On Drink* (New York: Harcourt Brace Jovanovich, 1973).

4. The phrase is W. J. Rorabaugh's. See his *The Alcoholic Republic: An American Tradition* (New York: Oxford University Press, 1979).

5. Dwight B. Heath, "A Decade of Development in the Anthropological Study of Alcohol Use: 1970–1980," in *Constructive Drinking: Perspectives on Drink from Anthropology*, ed. Mary Douglas (Cambridge: Cambridge University Press, 1987), 17.

6. Roland Barthes, "Wine and Milk," in *Mythologies*, trans. A. Lavers (New York: Hill and Wang, 1972), 58–61.

7. Alfred North Whitehead, *Symbolism: Its Meaning and Effect* (New York: Macmillan, 1927), 7–8.

8. Victor Turner, *The Forest of Symbols: Aspects of Ndembu Ritual* (Ithaca, N.Y.: Cornell University Press, 1967), 28.

9. Edward Sapir, "Symbolism," in *Encyclopaedia of the Social Sciences* (New York: Macmillan, 1934), 14:493.

10. Turner, *Forest of Symbols*. I have not been able to recuperate for my own purposes Turner's third and final property, "polarization of meaning," by which the symbol has both a moral and social meaning and also a natural and physiological one.

11. Dan Sperber, *Rethinking Symbolism*, trans. Alice L. Morton (Cambridge: Cambridge University Press, 1975), 33–34. I think that Turner was well aware of the problem. See Turner, *Forest of Symbols*, 45.

12. Pierre Bourdieu, *Distinction: A Social Critique of the Judgement of Taste*, trans. Richard Nice (Cambridge, Mass.: Harvard University Press, 1984).

13. Ibid., xii.

14. Ibid., 467.

15. Sapir, "Symbolism," 494.

16. John R. Hale, "The First Performance," *Saturday Evening Post*, 10 Apr. 1909, 37. The passage is quoted at greater length in Simple Message 3 n. 12.

17. Lowell Edmunds, *The Silver Bullet: The Martini in American Civilization* (Westport, Conn.: Greenwood, 1981), 138.

18. Barnaby Conrad III, *The Martini: An Illustrated History of an American Classic* (San Francisco: Chronicle Books, 1995), 59; David Strick, "The Martini," *Premiere*, Nov. 1997, 136.

19. Philip Larkin, *Required Writing: Miscellaneous Pieces, 1955–1982* (New York: Farrar, Straus & Giroux, 1984), 72. I do not quite understand "quinine," the medicinal uses of which are analgesic, antipyretic, and antimalarial. As a medicine, it is usually administered in the form of salts, and perhaps Larkin is referring to its taste.

20. The manual is O. H. Byron, *The Modern Bartender's Guide* (New York, 1884). The short story is Hidley Dhee, "A Daring Game," *Crescent*, 1 Aug. 1896 (quoted in Simple Message 3).

APPENDIX

1. Paul Gardner, *The Glass of Fredrick Carder* (New York: Crown, 1971), 198. Only approximate dating is possible.

2. Ibid.

3. Ibid., 197. No information is given with the catalogue drawing, but on 107 there is a photograph of the glass (Illus. 168), which is designated "crystal cocktail glass," and the height is given as 6¾ inches. The caption further states that the olive is applied in green and that "'Well' one more" is engraved. The glass belongs to a private collection, otherwise unspecified.

4. *Acorn* 3 (1992): 75ff.

5. Boston and Sandwich Glass Company, ca. 1874, in *Acorn* 3 (1992): 21ff.; two other O'Hara Glass Company catalogues; Bakewell, Pears, and Co. (Pittsburgh), ca. 1875; McKee and Brothers (Pittsburgh), 1880 (flared only).

6. I have seen not the postcards themselves but only a reproduction of three of them, drastically reduced in size, in a catalogue.

7. Gardner, *Glass of Fredrick Carder*, 191.

8. My source is a photograph accompanying Pilar Viladas, "Couture House," *New York Times Magazine*, 5 Oct. 1997, pt. 2 (Home Design), p. 44.

9. The cone-shaped bowl was also coming to be identified with the Manhattan (a subject that is even less clear to me than the Martini glass)—not inappropriately, considering their affinity. See discussion of early Martini recipes in "Historical Background of the Ambiguities."

10. Jean-Pierre Keller, *La galaxie Coca-Cola* (Geneva: Editions Noir, 1980), chap. 4, demonstrates a remarkable isomorphism of name, graphics, and bottle shape.

11. Max Rudin, "'There Is Something about a Martini,'" *American Heritage* 48, no. 4 (July–Aug. 1997): 40.

12. The drink poses problems for waiters, too. See Richard Flaste, "Waiter's Challenge: An Unspilled Martini," *New York Times*, 1 Oct. 1997, F10.

13. Barnaby Conrad III, *The Martini: An Illustrated History of an American Classic* (San Francisco: Chronicle Books, 1995), 112. Cf. "A great Martini should be like skinny-dipping in a Nordic lake with Greta Garbo" (110).

14. Adrienne Mayor, "Libation Titillation: Wine Goblets and Women's Breasts," *Studies in Popular Culture* 16 (1994): 61–71.

15. Conrad, *Martini*, 111.

16. Mayor, "Libation Titillation," 64.

INDEX

absinthe, 60, 133n5
Abt, Clark, 132n8a
Acheson, Dean, 3–4
Across the River and into the Trees (Hemingway), 52
Ade, George, 128n12
Adler, Renata, 53
advertisements, 59–60, 111–12; for cocktails, 54, 77; for gin, 19, 41, 61, 65, 73, 74; Martini glass in, 95, 112, 122; in *New Yorker*, 65; relationships in, 60, 92; toughness of Martini in, 65. *See also particular brands*
Aiken, Conrad, 43, 44
alcohol, 71–74, 76; as medicine, 77; studies of, 103–4
alcoholics, 42–43, 47–50, 51, 87, 103, 109
Alias Basil Willing (McCloy), 48
America, xv, 71, 76, 108, 132n4a; gin in, 74–75; and the Martini, xix, xxiv, 3–7, 33, 36, 68, 69, 99, 106; and Martini glass, 122; vermouth in, 78–79
American and Other Drinks (Engel), 81, 116
American Bartender (Laird), 116
American Exposition (1887), 82
The American Heritage Cookbook, 82
American Literary Realism, 108, 117
American Standards Association, 93–94
An American Tragedy (Dreiser), 28
American Ways of Life (Stewart), 75
Amis, Kingsley, 143n79
Amory, Cleveland, 53
anchovies, 60, 62
Anderson, Peter, 5
Anderson, Sherwood, xi, xii, xv
Angell, Roger, 50
anisette, 143n73
"Another Lycidas" (Aiken), 43–44
Apple, R. W., Jr., 4
aquavit, 143n73
aqua vitae, 86
Arensburg, Paul, xxiv
Aristotle, 85
Art Deco, 123, 131n1
Athens-Olympia Restaurant (Boston), 43
Auden, W. H., 25–26, 65, 107
Auntie Mame, 28–29

Babbitt (Lewis), 42, 65
Bacchanology, 103
Bachrach, Judy, xxi
Baker, Russell, 18, 127n3
Banning, Kendall, 82
Barnes, Albert, 116
Barroll, Tricia, xxii
The Bartender (Concklin), 116
The Bartender (Lamore), 116
bartender's guides, 115–17
Bartenders' International League of America, 17
Bartender's Ready Reference, 116
Barthelme, Donald, 12
Barthes, Roland, 71, 104, 105
baseball, 49–50, 133n21
Bassett, Gordon, 43, 84
The Beautiful and the Damned (Fitzgerald), 53
Beefeater Gin, 19, 27, 82, 86, 135n4a
beer, 13, 71, 72, 73, 126n15
Beeton, Isabella, 16, 117
Belmont Springs water, 61
Benchley, Robert, 9, 127n3
Benedictine, 83
Bengal Gin, 65
Beverage Literature: A Bibliography (Noling), 117
Bevin, Ernest, 3–4
the Bible, 86
bitters, 60, 75–76, 77, 85; in early cocktails, 79, 83, 84
Bombay Dry Gin, 73
Bombay Sapphire Gin, xxii, 112
Bond, James, 29, 65–66, 68, 69
The Book of Lists, 82
Boothby, William T., 80, 116
Booth's House of Lords gin, 61
Bourdieu, Pierre, 106, 107
Bradford, Sarah, 32
brandy, 72, 74, 76, 78
Brideshead Revisited (Waugh), 52
Brigham, Clarence, 64
Brighton (cocktail), 83
Briones, John M. ("Toddy"), 82
Bronx (cocktail), 69, 108, 128n12
Brown, Jared M., xxi, xxiv, 115
Buck, Pearl S., 5

Index

About the Author Lowell Edmunds is Professor of Classics at Rutgers University. Among his many books are works on Greek drama and myth, comparative folklore, and Roman poetry.

About the Artist Deborah Ellis's paintings and prints are included in numerous corporate and public collections, including those of the Library of Congress, the National Museum of Women in the Arts, and the *Washington Post*. She lives in Alexandria, Virginia, and in Maine.